D!RTY ®
ITALIAN

D!RTY®

ITALIAN

Everyday Slang from "What's Up?" to "F*%# Off!"

THIRD EDITION

GABRIELLE EUVINO

illustrated by **LINDSAY MACK**

Published by:
Ulysses Press
PO Box 3440
Berkeley, CA 94703
www.ulyssespress.com

ISBN13: 978-1-64604-261-6
Library of Congress Control Number: 2021937740

Printed in the United States by Kingery Printing Company
20 19 18 17 16 15 14

Managing editor: Claire Chun
Project editor: Kierra Sondereker
Proofreader: Barbara Schultz
Interior design: what!design @ whatweb.com
Cover design: Double R Design
Front cover photo: © clipart.com
Back cover illustration: Lindsay Mack
Interior art: Lindsay Mack except cocktail glass © Svitlana
Cocktail recipes: Katy Chapman and Chrissy McIntyre,
    The Barlingual Chicks

Special thanks to:
Laura Anson

for giving eyes to the angels.
Life without friends is nothing.
La vita senza l'amicizia è nulla.
(Cicero)

TABLE OF CONTENTS

USING
THIS BOOK

You may remember struggling to stay awake in your eighth-period high school *classe di italiano*. All those verb drills and conjugations, the teacher droning on and on, you doodling along the margins of your secondhand textbook. You skipped class, failed your tests, thought the period would never end. Who cares about *la grammatica* (grammar), *i verbi* (verbs), and *il vocabolario* (vocabulary) anyway?

Now, imagine what your *esperienza* could have been: Your textbook is a copy of *Dirty Italian*. The *maestra* (teacher) starts waving her arms and cursing, inciting the class to "*ripetete!*" Together you chant "*Testa di cazzo…Figlio di puttana…*" ("Dickhead…Son-of-a-bitch…")

Instead of politely raising your hand, you would be encouraged to interrupt with your best and worst *offese* (insults), and rather than being told not to talk in class, you would be given extra credit for swearing. And instead of being taught the verb "to be" over and over again, you would be given practical pickup lines for the cutie who sits across from you. It's doubtful you would have ever missed a class.

I assume you've picked up this book out of *curiosità*. Much of the material herein contained is inflammatory, crude, vulgar, and infantile, not to mention degrading, inflating, and

iTALiAN PRONUNCiATiON)))
LA PRONUNCIA ITALIANA

Per fortuna (lucky you), unlike English, Italian is a very reasonable language when it comes to figuring out the pronunciation. The first thing you should do is add a vowel to the end of every word. *No problema*! Just fake it till you make it!

Also in your favor is the fact that Italian and English share a lot of cognates; these are words that look and sound like each other (*banana, stupido, problema*, etc.) but are from different languages (like banana, stupid, problem, etc.). You'll see quite a few of them throughout the book.

Italian is a phonetically based language. Keep this basic rule in mind: What you see, you say. The Italian alphabet is just like the English alphabet minus the letters "j," "k," "w," "x," "y" (although they are used with foreign words and names). For example, both English and Italian possess the same "k" sound, but utilize different letters to get there. Think of Chianti wine and you begin to get it.

The vowels are pronounced:

a sounds like "ah," as in "bra"

e sounds like "eh," as in "sex"

i sounds like "ee," as in "orgy"

o sounds like "oh," as in "blow"

u sounds like "oo," as in "nude"

There are no silent letters in Italian with the exception of any word that begins with "h," such as "hotel" (pronounced *oh-tel*).

Certain letter combinations differ from English and include:

ch is pronounced like "k," as in Chianti

ci is like the "ch" sound in English, as in *ciao*

ce also sounds like "ch," as in *centro* (pronounced *CHEN-troh*)

ge is pronounced like a "j," as in genitalia

insulting. Let's face it, if you want to sound like an *Italiano*, you have to learn how to swear like one. For Italians, *gergo* (slang) and curses serve as punctuation between thoughts and ideas. Slang is used everywhere by pretty much everyone.

gi also sounds like a "j," as in *vagina*

gh is pronounced like it's used in English in words like *ghetto* (an Italian word)

gn sounds like "ni" like the word "companion," as in *bagno* (pronounced *BAHN-yoh*) and *gnocchi* (pronounced *NYOHK-kee*)

oi is pronounced "oy," as in *troia*

r is very lightly trilled

rr should sound like the purr of a pussycat—just don't overdo it.

s sounds like the "s" in "sex," as in *sesso* (pronounced *SES-soh*) when it begins a word, but if it's inside a word it sounds more like a "**z**," as in *casa* (pronounced *KAH-zah*).

sc + the vowels "a," "o," and "u" is pronounced with a hard "k" sound (*scandolo, scopare, scusa*)

sc + the vowels "e" and "i" are pronounced with a soft "sh" sound like *pesce* (pronounced *PEH-sheh*), and *sci* (pronounced like "she")

Take your double consonants seriously: always linger on them a little longer—*pene* means "penis"...*penne* is the pasta (it's also the word for "pens"). *Capheesh?*

Don't stress out about where to put the emphasis in Italian. Although there are exceptions, in general, with words of two syllables the first syllable should be slightly stressed. For example, the word *merda* (shit) would be pronounced *mer-dah*. With longer words, the stress is generally placed on the second-to-last syllable; the verb *incazzare* (to piss off) is pronounced *een-katz-ZAH-reh*. Exceptions include whenever you see an accent, such as in *città* (city), pronounced *cheet-TAH*.

The best way to learn *la bella lingua italiana*, of course, is to hook up with an Italian. This book could be the start of a long and lasting relationship, if you play your *carte* right.

Italians are by nature irreverent. They can be a lot of things, including rude, mean, spiteful, pissy, and bitchy. But let's not forget they're also some of the most kind, generous, original, creative, and gifted poets, writers, artists, scientists, musicians, mathematicians, dancers, thinkers, philosophers, students, and teachers the world has ever known.

Hell, Italians invented half the shit you take for granted. They gave the world ball bearings, banks, batteries, and the dictionary; they created espresso machines, highways, hydrofoils, and the first internal combustion engine; they invented liposuction, the mile, musical notation, parachutes, perfumes, pianos, pistols, and polymers. They gave us artificial insemination, cloning, and condoms. *Grazie* to the Italians, you can listen to talk radio and telephone your BFF. Italians gave us the stiletto, the *violino*, and the water bed. Let's not forget *vino*, vermouth, and oh yeah, nuclear fuckin' reactors.

Italian is kind of like Latin's little bastard child. Whatever name it takes, the relationship is undeniable. Think about the Roman poet Ovid (c. 43 BC–AD 17) and his work *Ars Amatoria* ("The Art of Love"); two thousand years later, the book still holds its own on the art of seduction. Italian was called a vulgar language because it was spoken by the common folk. Writers like Dante, Machiavelli, and Shakespeare all drew inspiration from that same "vulgar" vocabulary.

So now you, too, can draw from this vulgarly romantic language. Without some guidance, though, it can be very tough for the non-native speaker to distinguish the straight stuff from the smut. To the foreigner, the string of profanities that come pouring out of Italians' mouths sound like one run-on sentence, which essentially it is: *brutto-deficienteincapace-stupido-coglione-testa di cazzo-pezzo di merda-faccia da culo-presuntuoso vigliacco...* ("ugly-dimwitimpotent-stupid-idiot-dickhead-piece of shit-assface-presumptuous coward..."). At least now you'll understand it!

iTALiAN GRAMMAR)))
LA GRAMMATICA ITALIANA

I know, grammar schmammar. But it doesn't hurt to have quick primer on what's what. You learned all this shit once, but you were probably too bored, pent up, and horny to pay *attenzione*. So here it is again, even if not much has changed since middle school.

Italian nouns work like French and Spanish nouns—every noun has a gender, either masculine or feminine. Most Italian nouns require the use of the definite article. The singular articles are *il*, which is used in front of most masculine nouns, like *il figo* (the hottie); *la*, which is used in front of most feminine nouns, like *la fanciulla* (the chick); *l'*, used in front of any noun that begins with a vowel, like *l'ignorante* (the ignoramus); and *lo*, used in front of a masculine noun that begins with a "z" or with an "s" plus a consonant, like *lo scemo* (the fool). The plural definite articles include *i*, *gli*, and *le*.

Adjectives must agree with the nouns they modify. Whenever you see words like *bello/a* (beautiful) or *brutto/a* (ugly), the "/a" is there to remind you that you need to change your adjective if the subject is feminine. Foreign words like "sexy" remain the same whether you're speaking about a man or a woman.

> *George Clooney è bello.*
>
> *Monica Bellucci è bella.*

Possessives follow the same act as adjectives and always reflect the gender and number of the thing(s) being possessed, like when you say *Mamma mia*.

Consider *Dirty Italian* as a *libretto* for cussing in Italian. In this *edizione*, I've reorganized and updated the material, keeping the best stuff and adding more of the sultry.

This book includes the most commonly uttered popular slogans and swears used by the general *popolazione* (population) but there's plenty to be discovered once you hook into an Italian *locale* (hangout) and start talking the talk (along with sixty million other people). Never mind the dialects for now. The standard Italian—spoken at work and school, on buses, and in train stations, airports, and

TO BE OR NOT TO BE: THE VERB ESSERE)))

In order to judge people, you're going to want to have a basic understanding of the verb *essere* (to be). Calling someone a "dumbass" will be a lot more effective if you can avoid saying, "You is a dumbass."

I am	*io sono*
you are	*tu sei*
he is	*lui*
she is	*lei*
we are	*noi siamo*
you are (plural)	*voi siete* (in other words, "you guys")
they are	*loro sono*

DIMINUTIVES AND SUPERLATIVES

Italian allows speakers to modify nouns and adjectives by using diminutives and superlatives. Some useful adapters include:

-accio typically gives a negative connotation to something

un tipo, un tipaccio (a dude, a jerkoff)

-etto makes things more familiar and cuter

il culo, il culetto (the ass, the cute ass)

-ino makes nouns and adjectives smaller or less than

il gatto, il gattino (the cat, the kitten)

piccolo/a, piccolino/a (small, eensy-weensy)

-issimo exaggerates adjectives

bello/a, bellissimo/a (beautiful, gorgeous)

-one makes things bigger

il cazzo, il cazzone (the dick, the big dick)

supermarkets—has more smutty, dirty, filthy, wash-out-your-mouth-with-soap words than you could ever need. While you shouldn't expect to be quoting Dante here, you'll certainly be able to describe *che merdaio* (what a shithole) hell can be.

Attenzione: Even though *Dirty Italian* is designed to offer you all the sleaze you could ever please, misuse of this book could result in the loss of *amici* (friends), *amanti* (lovers), and your sweet *culo* (ass). Don't blame me if you end up homeless, friendless, or locked up because you pissed off the wrong person at the wrong time. Words don't necessarily insult people—people do. Now take this book and get dirty!

CHAPTER 1

HOWDY ITALIAN
SALU TI ITALIANI

Before you can get *veramente* (very) dirty in Italy, you're going to need to warm up a little. Italian small talk is the equivalent of linguistic foreplay, the *antipasto*, or the meal before the meal. Stretch your *lingua* (tongue) with these common Italian greetings and ice breakers.

••••Breakin' the ice
Rompere il ghiaccio

Ciao has become a popular way of greeting friends all over the world. (Dude, please get the spelling right: It's written c-i-a-o, and not c-h-o-w like you would order in a Chinese restaurant.) Italians are notorious for their flatteries. No one ever minds if you add *bello* or *bella* after this little word.

Hi / bye!
Ciao!

Hi handsome/beautiful!
Ciao bello/a!

Hi gorgeous!
Ciao bellissimo/a!

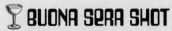

🍸 BUONA SERA SHOT

Who needs a shot of espresso when you can kick-start your morning with a bit of coffee liqueur, rum, and amaretto? *Sì grazie!*

GET THESE:
- ½ ounce amaretto
- ½ ounce coffee liqueur
- ½ ounce white rum

DO THIS:
Put all the ingredients into a cocktail shaker with ice. Shake until well chilled and strain into a shot glass. Down in one gulp or take your time.

Whatcha' up to?
Cosa fai?

How's it goin'?
Come va?

Hey boss!
Capo!

Good morning!
Buon giorno!
This is used to mean both "good morning" and "good day."

Good evening!
Buona sera!
This is used in the afternoon and evening when greeting people, as well as to say "good-bye."

It's a beautiful day! / evening!
Bella giornata! / serata!

Good night!
Buona notte!

There are two ways of asking someone their name, politely or familiarly:

What's your name? (polite)
Come si chiama?

What do you go by? (familiar)
Come ti chiami?

Do you speak English?
Parla l'inglese?

Or, switch out the existing question with this:

Do you speak English? (polite)
Parli l'inglese?

·····How are ya?
Come stai?

What's up?
Che c'è?

What's the word?
Tutto bene?

How are ya?
Come stai?

What's good?
Cosa c'è di bello?

What's happening?
Che si dice?

What's new?
Cosa c'è di nuovo?

Any news?
Novità?

How's it goin'?
Come va?

> **Can't complain.**
> *Non mi lamento.*

> **Eh...**
> *Beh...*

DiALOGUE))
IL DIALOGO

My name is Bernice.
Mi chiamo Bernice.

I'm from the United States and I like men with big guns.
Vengo dagli Stati Uniti e mi piacciono gli uomini con le pistole grandi.

Can you show me where I can find a bar to get toasted with all my American friends?
Mi puoi indicare dov'è un bar per ubricarmi con i miei amici americani?

I'm Chad.
Sono Chad.

I have a really shitty accent.
Ho un accento proprio di merda.

Will you help me study? I have a really quiet room with a very comfortable bed.
Mi puoi aiutare a studiare? Ho una stanza molto silenziosa con un letto comodissimo.

Everything's cool.
Tutto a posto.
Literally, "Everything in place."

Fantastic!
Fantastico!

Getting by.
Mi arrangio.

Good!
Bene!

You work with what you've got.
Si arrangia con quello che c'è.
From the verb *arrangiarsi* (to deal with things). *L'arte di arrangiarsi* describes "the art of figuring shit out."

Good enough!
Benone!

Great!
Benissimo!

TiTLes))
TITOLI

Italians address strangers the way we used to in the U.S., back in the day when Americans were polite, using Mr. or Mrs. or Miss. Always err on the side of too formal, especially when meeting *i genitori* (the parents) of your new Italian friend.

Mr.
Signore
> It's nice to meet you, Mr. Ciula.
> *E' un piacere conoscer La, Signor Ciula.*

Mrs./Ms.
Signora
> It's a pleasure to make your acquaintance, Mrs. Troia.
> *E' un piacere fare la Sua conoscenza, Signora Troia.*

Miss
Signorina
> Excuse me miss, but have we met?
> *Mi scusi signorina, ma ci siamo già conosciuti?*

Hanging in there.
Me la cavo.
From the verb *cavarsela* (to manage).

Not bad.
Mica male.

Shitty.
Di merda.

So-so.
Così-così.

Whatever...
Insomma…

How's it hanging?
Che aria tira?

It's better if you don't ask.
Meglio che non me lo chiedi.

What do you care?
Che te ne importa?

·····See you soon!
A presto!

If you've ever spent *le feste* (the holidays) with an Italian *famiglia*, you know that Italian good-byes can take as long as the visit itself.

Take care!
Prenditi cura!

Be well!
Stammi bene!

See you!
Ci vediamo!

Maybe I'll catch you in the piazza later on?
Ci troviamo più'tardi in piazza, magari?

Good night!
Buona notte!

Later!
A più tardi!

See ya tomorrow.
A domani.

I can't wait!
Non vedo l'ora!
Literally, "I don't see the hour."

Good-bye!
Arrivederci!

Call me!
Chiamami!

Text me!
Mandami un SMS!
Pronounced *ess-ay em-ay ess-ay*.

I gotta bounce.
Devo andarmene.

I'm outta here.
Me ne vado.

Peace!
Pace!

·····How's life treating you?
Come ti va la vita?

One of the coolest things about an Italian city is *la piazza*, essentially the town square. It's where Italians go to ogle one another, to show off their good looks, and to meet up before going out. Look for a marble cherub pissing into a *fontana* or some bronze *statua* of a dead poet or soldier and you'll know you're there.

Trying to find your way around the maze of *strade* (roads) in an Italian town or city can be a total nightmare. If you don't know how to find a *piazza*, follow the bull's-eye symbol toward *centro* ("center," or downtown) and you'll find one for sure.

Hey!
Ehi!

Look who's coming!
Guarda chi c'è!

Damn! How long has it been?
Accidenti! Da quanto tempo non ti vedo?

How's your wifey/hubby?
Come sta la tua mogliettina/il tuo maritino?

Long time no see!
Non ci vediamo da tanto tempo!

Nice running into you.
Sono felice di vederti.
Literally, "I'm happy to see you."

What a pleasure to see you!
Che piacere vederti!

What've you been up to?
Che hai combinato?

Where've you been?
Dove sei stato/a?

·····Please and thank you
Per favore e grazie

Please!
Per favore!

Pleez!
Per piacere!

Thanks.
Grazie.

Thanks a million.
Mille grazie.

Thanks a lot.
Tante grazie.

Thanks for fuckin' nothing.
Grazie al cazzo!

Don't mention it.
Non c'è di che.

You're welcome.
Prego.
Like *ciao*, *prego* is another multipurpose word that can
mean a lot more than "you're welcome." It also means
"no prob," "after you," "make yourself comfortable," and
"cool." When Italians say *Ti prego!*? they're really saying "I'm
beggin' ya!" or "You gotta do me this favor!"

It's nothing.
Non fa niente.

Who gives a damn?!
Chi se ne frega?!

Excuse me.
Mi scusi.

'Scuse me.
Scusami.

Capeesh?
Hai capito?

I get it.
Ho capito.

I'm with ya.
Ti capisco.
Literally, "I understand."

I'm following.
Ti seguo.

Sorry.
Mi dispiace.

My bad!
Mea culpa!

My fault!
Colpa mia!

Oops!
Ops!

It's totally my fault!
È tutta colpa mia!

I messed up big time!
Ho cannato alla grande.

What a fuck-up!
Che puttanata!
From the word *puttana* (whore).

Forgive me, man.
Scusami, amico.

My sincere apologies.
Chiedo scusa.

·····Let's talk weather
Parliamo del tempo

Why do Italians talk about *il tempo* (the weather)? Because even if you have absolutely nothing else in common, you're both alive and breathing, standing underneath the same sky. It's a start. There's nothing like talking about how shitty the weather is to break an awkward *silenzio*.

What's the weather like?
Che tempo fa?

It's...
È...

a nice day.
una bella giornata.

nice out.
bello.

bleak.
brutto.

shitty out today.
una merda oggi.

a really shitty day.
proprio una giornata di merda.

It's hot as hell.
Fa un caldo infernale.

It's fuckin' hot.
*C'è **un caldo bestiale**.*
Literally, "a beastly heat."

The weather sucks.
Il tempo fa schifo.

It's not that bad.
Non è poi così brutto.

It's cold.
Fa freddo.

It's cold as balls.
Fa un freddo cane.
Literally, "It's dog cold."

What's up with the fucking rain today?
Ma che cazzo piove oggi?

·····Do I know you?
Ci conosciamo?

It may seem like the most obvious pickup line in the book, but it works like a friggin' charm. The next time you want to *abbordare* (pick up) an Italian *figa* (babe), pretend like you're long-lost amici (friends). Start with *Ciao, ti ricordi di me*? (Hey, do you remember me?). Now you've put her in the hot seat; stand there with an eager grin. If she still doesn't remember (which of course, she won't), offer her reminders. *Forse la festa di Stefano*? *Una vita passata*? (Maybe Stefano's party? A past life?)

You're leaving already? Can I come with you?
Vai già via? Posso accompagnarti?

Can I give you a hand?
Posso darti una mano?

Can I offer you a drink?
Posso offrirti qualcosa da bere?

Can you light me up?
Hai d'accendere?

Are you from around here?
Sei di qua?

Wanna go out sometime?
Ti va di uscire insieme qualche volta?

Can I get your…?
Posso avere il tuo…?

GOOD LUCK!)))
BUONA FORTUNA!

During Roman times, bloodthirsty spectators chanted in Latin *quasso crusis* (break a leg) to wish the gladiators good luck. The expression actually refers to the bending of one's leg, hopefully to pick up the money that audiences used to pelt their favorite players with, or later, flowers thrown onto the stage.

Given their general cynicism, Italians are known for their *superstizioni* (superstitions) and have developed quite a few methods to ward off *maledizioni* (curses), including the *malocchio* (evil eye). Some believe that if you wish them good luck, you're inviting bad luck (the same reason you always tell an actor to "break a leg.")

What fuckin' luck!
Che culo!
Literally, "what ass."

You're a lucky son-of-a-bitch!
Che culo che hai!
Literally, "What an ass you have!"

Best of luck!
In bocca al lupo!
Literally, "In the mouth of the wolf."
This is used especially when you're not quite sure of a situation's outcome and can use all the positive vibes you can get. The Italians will get a kick out of hearing you say the expected response to this: *Crepi il lupo*! (*Crepi* figuratively means "die.")

Kick ass!
In culo alla balena!
Literally, "Up the ass of the whale!" Here, the appropriate response would be: *Speriamo che non caghi*! ("Here's hoping he doesn't shit!") Probably adapted from the biblical story of Jonah and the whale.

What shit luck!
Che sfiga!

number
numero di telefono

address
indirizzo

I wanna see you **this evening**.
*Voglio vederti **stasera**.*

Who are you, where did you come from, and where are you going?
***Chi se**i, da dove vieni, e dove vai?*

It feels like I've known you **forever**.
*Mi sento di conoscerti da **sempre**.*

You look just like the first girl I ever fell in love with.
Assomigli tanto alla prima ragazza di cui mi sono innammorato.

Do you want to go out or should I just go fuck myself?
Vuoi uscire o vado a farmi fottere?

And for the ladies who are sick of hearing the same cliché B.S....

Sorry, I'm **engaged**.
*Mi dispiace, sono **fidanzata**.*

Don't take it personally; I'm a **lesbian**.
*Non te la prendere; sono **lesbica**.*

I don't see you that way, but I hope we can stay **friends**.
*Non ti vedo in quella maniera, ma spero di rimanere **amici**.*

You can't imagine how much I value you and your **friendship**.
*Tu non immagini quanto tengo a te e alla tua **amicizia**.*

You're kidding, right?
***Scherzi**, vero?*

WOW!))
WOW!

Italians are known for their *passione* and enthusiasm. Any of the following are used to say "Wow!"

Wow!
Ammappa!
Used mostly in central Italy.

Hot damn!
Ammazza!
Used throughout Italy to express incredulity.

Fucking A!
Cacchio!
The word also refers to a weiner.

Man! Holy shit!
Caspita!

Fuck yeah!
Cazzo!
Literally means "dick" and is on the extreme of the vulgar scale...which doesn't stop millions of Italians from using it every day.

Win!
Cavolo!
A euphemism for *cazzo* and literally translates to "cabbage."

Incredible!
Incredibile!

Woot!
Mamma mia!
Literally, "my mother."

I'm not that **desperate**!
*Non sono mica così **disperata**!*

What **planet** are you from?
*Ma da che **pianeta** vieni?*

When hell freezes over!
Non sono ancora alla frutta!
Literally, "I'm still not at the fruit," the last part of a meal.

·····What a mess
Che pasticcio

Just because Italians live in a country that often looks like a scene out of a *favola* (fairy tale) doesn't mean they're always living one. Even with one of the most gorgeous populations on the *pianeta* (planet) combined with the most delish *piatti* (dishes) your palate could ever hope for, shit happens. Traffic jams, flat tires, strikes, fires, heartbreaks, deaths, illness, mullets...not everything is a picnic in Italy. Commiserate with your *compari*.

> **What...**
> *Che...*
>
>> **craziness!**
>> *casino!*
>>
>> **a disaster!**
>> *disastro!*
>>
>> **madness!**
>> *pasticcio!*
>>
>> **a shame!**
>> *peccato!*
>>
>> **a scam!**
>> *imbroglio!*
>>
>> **a scene!**
>> *chiassata!*
>>
>> **a bitch!**
>> *bordello!*
>> Literally, "brothel."
>>
>> **trouble!**
>> *guaio!*

▪▪▪▪▪You're kidding!
Ma stai scherzando!

There are a lot of words and exclamations used to express that we're totally with someone when they're speaking. In English, we say things like "No way!" and "I hear you." Believe me, if you toss out some of these *espressioni*, you'll have everyone convinced that you understand way more than you actually do.

Are you kidding?
Scherzi?

Are you shitting me?
Mi stai prendendo per il culo?
Literally, "You're taking me for an ass."

I don't believe it.
Non ci credo.

For real?
Davvero?

Seriously?
Sul serio?

No shit!
Dai!

Yeah right!
Ma va'!

Check it out.
Che roba.
Literally, "What stuff."

Come on!
Ma dai!

Exactly.
Appunto.

For sure.
Di sicuro.

SHUT UP!))

STA' ZITTO!

Italians are hardly known to politely wait for their turn to speak. When five people are talking at the same time, it can sometimes seem like it's more about who can talk the longest and the loudest than about actually communicating.

Be quiet!
Taci!

Shut up, fuckhead!
Sta' zitto/a, testa di cazzo!

Hear me out.
Ascoltami.

Listen.
Senti.

Out with it.
Di'.

Pay attention to me.
Dammi retta.

Shut your trap!
Chiudi il becco!
Literally, "Close your beak."

Spill it!
Dimmi!
Literally, "Tell me!"

Tell me everything.
Dimmi tutto.

Get outta here!
Sparisci!

I agree.
D'accordo.

I understand.
Capisco.

No way!
Non me lo dire...ma vah!

Totally.
Assolutamente.

Without a doubt.
Senza dubbio.

Word!
Per Bacco!
Literally, "For Bacchus!"

You know it.
Sai com'è.

Crazy!
Pazzesco!

Damn!
Accidenti!

Horrible!
Orribile!

Scandalous!
Scandaloso!

SO?)))
ALL ORA?

Allora is one of those words you'll hear over and over again and which serves as the Italian word for "ummmmmmmm..." It can also mean "so," "then," "like," and "thus," among a million other things. You'll also hear *comunque* and *dunque*, used to express "So, like I was sayin'..."

> So-so
> *Così-così*
> *Così* also means "so" as in *Sono così innamorato/a!* (I'm soooo in love!) and is used to say "so-so," generally in *risposta* to the query *Come va?* (How's it goin'?)

Seductive!
Seducente!

You're crazy!
Sei pazzo/a!

You're nuts!
Sei matto/a!

You're pulling my leg.
Mi prendi in giro.
Literally, "You're taking me for a spin."

You're out of your mind.
Sei fuori.

How come?
Come mai?

Who knows?
Chissà?

Yep.
Eh già.
This translates to "already," but is used when someone has stated the obvious.

I swear.
Ti giuro.

If only!
Magari!
Italians use this to express something desirable that's probably never gonna happen, like "Yeah, when pigs fly!"

••••Who?
Chi?

You don't have to speak perfect Italian to get by—these little question words can help you score a lot of points. After all, you've got to know *dove* (where) and *quando* (when) it's time to meet up.

Who is that hot babe?
Chi è quella figa?

What the fuck are you doing?
Che cazzo fai?
Che cosa is also used to mean "what" in a lot of cases.

When are you going to take off your pants?
Quando ti togli i pantaloni?

Why don't we have a quickie right here?
Perché non ci facciamo una sveltina qui in questo momento?

How do you like it?
Come ti piace?

Wait! You've done it with **how many** people?
Aspetta! Con quante persone l'hai fatto?

Where did your pants go?
Dove sono andati i tuoi pantaloni?

┈┉Best wishes!
Auguri!

Even if you're completely depressed, have run out of Prozac, and are feeling slightly suicidal, do everyone a favor: Suck it up and pretend to be *allegro/a* (happy) for someone else.

Best wishes!
Auguri!

Congrats!
Congratulazioni!

Happy birthday!
Buon compleanno!

Happy holidays!
Buone feste!

Well done!
Ben fatto!

Awesome!
Mitico!

Charming!
Grazioso!

Compliments!
Complimenti!

Fabulous!
Favoloso!

Fantastic!
Fantastico!

Sweet!
Che figata!

Way to go!
Eh vai!

What a blast!
Che bomba!

CHAPTER 2

FRIENDLY ITALIAN

ITALIANO AMICHEVOLE

The best way to learn friendly Italian is to sit at the nearest café and listen to the melodious chitter-chatter. Italians are known for their banter, where ribbing, gossiping, and teasing are all forms of demonstrating their affection for both friends and *famiglia*. Italians don't beat around the bush—if they want to know you better, they'll ask you for all sorts of personal *informazione*. Be prepared to answer, and don't hold back if you've got a question or two yourself. Being direct is appreciated (most of the time).

•••••Flirting
Flirtare

In the old days, a single young woman was called *nubile* (from "nubile"), while an unwed male was referred to as *celibe* (from "celibate"). Once the strays started growing on her unmarried chin, she became *una zitella* (an old maid); when his ears begun to sprout hair, he was simply deemed *uno scapolo* (a bachelor). Today, Italians simply describe themselves as either *sposato/a* (married), or *non sposato/a* (not married).

♈ APEROL SPRITZ

Greet your *famiglia* at the door with an aperol spritz. They won't notice all the dust bunnies and your inept attempts to clean when they're tipsy.

GET THESE:

 3 ounces Aperol

 3 ounces prosecco

 1 ounce club soda

 orange slice, for garnish

DO THIS:

Fill a large wine glass with ice. Add the Aperol and top with the prosecco and club soda. Slide the orange inside the glass and press it against the side so it's really pretty and it looks like you made an effort.

The English word "single" is also used, but with an Italian accent it would sound more like *seen-gol*.

Do you live alone?
Vivi da solo/a?

Do you have a girlfriend?
Hai una ragazza?

This is my boyfriend.
Questo è il mio ragazzo.
A quick note about Italian grammar and possessives: The "my" part reflects the gender of the thing that is being possessed. *La mia* is used in front of feminine nouns and il mio is used in front of masculine nouns.

This is my girlfriend.
Questa è la mia ragazza.

We're basically engaged.
Siamo praticamente fidanzati.

Are you married?
*Sei **sposato/a**?*

I'm …
Sono…

> **single.**
> *single.*
>
> **married.**
> *sposato/a.*
>
> **divorced.**
> *divorziato/a.*
>
> **widowed.**
> *vedovo/a.*

Where's your hubby?
*Dov'è il tuo **maritino**?*

Where's your wifey?
*Dov'è la tua **moglietta**?*

We're separated.
*Ci siamo **separati**.*

How old are you?
Quanti anni hai?

I'm eighteen.
*Ho **diciotto** anni.*

·····Friends or fuck-buddies?
Amici o trombamici?

You might be an island of *indipendenza* and self-reliance, but Italians like to really connect. They hang out in *gruppi* and make new friends through existing ones. This works out well for foreigners, because once you've made the acquaintance of one Italian, it's only a matter of time before you're warming up to his or her entire clan.

> **Do you like unicorns? Let's be friends.**
> *Ti piacciono gli unicorni? Facciamo amicizia.*

He/She's…
Lui/Lei è…

> **a friend.**
> *un amico/un'amica.*

> **a close friend.**
> *un amico/un'amica d'intimo.*

> **a really tight friend.**
> *un amico/un'amica di ferro.*
> Literally, "an iron friend."

> **my best friend.**
> *il mio migliore amico/la mia migliore amica.*

> **my BFF.**
> *il mio amico/la mia amica del cuore.*
> Literally, "friend of the heart."

> **my blood.**
> *il mio amico/la mia amica per la pelle.*
> Literally, "my skin brother/sister."

> **a bosom buddy.**
> *un amico/un'amica cilegia.*
> Literally, "a cherry friend," from the fact that when you
> pick cherries, they come in pairs.

> **a soulmate.**
> *un'anima gemella.*

> **my fuck-buddy.**
> *il mio compagno/la mia compagna di trombate.*

> **a friend with benefits.**
> *un po' più di un amico/un'amica.*
> Literally, "a little more than a friend."

> **a buddy.**
> *un/a compagno/a.*

> **roommate.**
> *un/a compagno/a di camera.*

> **classmate.**
> *un/a compagno/a di scuola.*

> **playmate.**
> *un/a compagno/a di giochi.*

a partner. (as in live-in)
un/a convivente.

a pen pal.
un amico/un'amica di penna.

an acquaintance.
un/una conoscente.

a coworker.
un/a collega

a frenemy.
un amico/un'amica del giaguaro.
Literally, "a jaguar friend," someone who pretends to be
your friend.

·····Hey, dude.
Ciao, amico.

Although there doesn't appear to be a universally accepted
translation of "Hey, dude" in Italian, it's safe to say *Ciao,
amico* ("Hiya, friend") is a pretty close fit. In different dialects, Italians also throw around *ciccio* (Tuscany), *zio*
(Milan), *cumpà* (southern Italy), or *cocco* (Central Italy).

In the good old days, many Italian-American communities
used the word *paesan* (short for *paesano*) to indicate a
buddy or mate. These aren't the old days. If you wanna
sound like Tony Soprano, go ahead and use it. Otherwise,
stick with *amico* (friend) or *fratello* (brother).

Bro
Fra'

Brother
Fratello
Literally, "brother," but also used to indicate a friend.

Homey
Compagno
Literally, "countryman."

How's it goin' homey?
*Come va **compagno**?*

Friend
Amico

Hey, friend!
*Ciao, **amico**!*
Amico is also used to address someone as dude.

Dude
Tipo

> **That dude at the club was so whack.**
> *Quel **tipo** al club era folle.*

Guy
Tizio

> **I met some guy whose name I can't remember.**
> *Ho conosciuto un **tipo** il cui nome non mi ricordo.*

Homeboy
Compare ; Compaesano

> **How's life treating you, homeboy?**
> *Come ti va la vita, **compare**?*

·····All mine
Tutto mio/Tutta mia

Hey, you own what you lay claim to; let everyone know just what the situation is. Make sure it's clear you two are an item before someone comes along and steals your girl (or

man) away. If you haven't noticed, you've got a lot of com-
petizione out there.

I'm yours.
Sono tuo/tua.

This is…
Questo/a è…

> my **lover.**
> *il mio/la mia amante.*

> my **lovah.**
> *il mio/la mia innamorato/a.*

> my **man.**
> *il mio uomo.*

> my **woman,**
> *la mia donna.*

> my **partner.**
> *il mio/la mia partner.*
> *Compagno/a* is also used.

We've been together for five months.
Siamo insieme da cinque mesi.

·····Family
La Famiglia

In North America, we tend to date first, and then—if things
are going well—we meet the *famiglia*. Not necessarily
so in *Italia*. Your first date with an Italian could very well
involve an introduction to the entire clan. By the way, there
is no specific word in Italian for the word "date"—you
make an *appuntamento* (literally, "appointment"). If you
make the grade, you can have a second date. Here's a
little tip to remember: never arrive at someone's home
empty-handed. Bring flowers, pastries, or a bottle of wine.
Otherwise, they'll smile and tell you *Non c'è nessun problema* (It's not a problem), but once you're outta there, you
can bet they'll be talking mad shit about you.

Family friend
Amico/a di famiglia

Father
Padre

Daddy
Papà
The final accented à should be stressed to distinguish it
from the word *papa* (pope); not to be confused with the
word *pappa* (baby mush).

Pops
Babbo

Mother
Madre

Mom
Mamma

Husband
Marito

Wife
Moglie

Brother
Fratello

Little brother
Fratellino

Sister
Sorella

Little sister
Sorellina

Fiancé
Fidanzato/a
Even if you're not planning on tying the knot anytime
soon, the term *fidanzato/a* is used to describe your special
squeeze.

Cousin
Cugino/a

Uncle/Aunt
Zio/a

Auntie
Comare
This is the "auntie" that's not really related but gets the title because she's schtupping your uncle. This is technically dialect; it's commonly heard in movies and among Italian-American families.

·····Chromosome X
Cromosoma X

La femmina (female) comes in all shapes and sizes, but after centuries of war and peace (and a Renaissance and an Enlightenment, as well), the iconic *Italiana* has nurtured and cultivated an attitude that comes across in everything she does. She takes no prisoners—buyer beware.

A chica
Una tipa giusta

A chick
Una fanciulla

A gal
Una tipa

A girl
Una ragazza

A good girl
Una ragazza tutta casa e chiesa
Literally, "a girl who is all home and church."

Daddy's little girl
Una buona

A saint
Una santa
A variation of *santa*, *santina* is also used in the sarcastic expression *faccia da santina senza aureola* ("face of a little saint without the halo").

A school girl
Uno zainetto
Zainetto refers to the *zaino* (backpack) that all teenage girls carry.

A sweet girl
Una ragazza acqua e sapone
Literally, "a girl who's soap and water."

A dish
Una valida
Literally, "A valid."

A blabbermouth
Una chiacchierona

A single mother
Una ragazza madre

A cougar
Una tardona

An old lady
Una vecchia signora

A wild bitch
Una selvaggia

A man-eater
Una iena
Literally, "a hyena."

A wild horse
Una cavalla

A witch
Una strega

momism)))
IL MAMMISMO

Il mammismo is a decidedly Italian concept that refers to the tendency of unmarried adult male children to remain dependent on their mommies for most of their domestic needs. Extremely high youth unemployment and limited digs are mostly to blame for the fact that more than 50 percent of Italian males aged 18 to 34 still live at *casa* ("home," one of the most important words in the Italian language), yet no one seems to mind too much. If you're an American guy dating an Italian girl, you'll win a lot of points just by the fact you have been conditioned to take your own *piatto* (plate) to the sink and actually wash your own stinking underwear.

> Sure he's cute, but what a mamma's boy.
> *Sì, lui è carino, ma che **mammone**.*
>
> What a crybaby!
> *Che **figlio** di mamma!*

·····Chromosome Y
Cromosoma Y

Il maschio italiano isn't as easy to define as stereotyping would have you believe. He's even an enigma to himself.

A boy
Un ragazzo

An unlucky bastard
An poveraccio
Someone who's down on their luck.

A sugar daddy
Un papà-amante
Literally, "a daddy-lover." This term refers to a much older male lover.

A newbie
Un giovane
Literally, "young."

An animal
Un animale

A beast
Una bestia

A boy toy
Un uomo più giovane

A Casanova
Un uomo galante

A gigolo
Un gigolò

A Guido
Un birro
Incidentally, in Italy, Guido is simply a name and doesn't have the same negative connotation as it does among Italian-Americans. You'll know its equivalent, a *birro*, when you see one: sun-glasses even when it's raining, good-looking (in a Ken-doll kinda way), gold cross hanging from a chain, and when he's not working on his pecs, he's at the tanning booth. The typical Jersey Shore stereotype.

A baller
Un donnaiolo

A playboy
Uno stallone
Literally, "stallion."

A pimp
Un magnaccio/a

A player
Un ganzo

A jock
Un tipo sportivo

A metrosexual
Un metrosessuale

A mooch
Uno scroccone

A nerd
Uno sfigato

A pussy
Un coniglio
Literally, "a rabbit."

A sex maniac
Un maniaco sessuale

A tough cookie
Un tipo tosto

A trickster
Un truffatore

·····Characters
I tipi

Take one look at someone's *scarpe* (shoes) in Italy and you'll know instantly whether you're dealing with una *persona sfigata* (a loser) or a punk.

A punk (related to music)
Un/a punk

A rocker
Un/a rockettaro/a

A hick
Un/a campagnolo/a

A hippie
Un/a hippie

A hustler
Un/a imbroglione/a

A fucker
Un fottitore/una fottitrice

A phony
Un/a falsone/a

A gold digger
Un cacciatore/una cacciatrice di dote

A Goody-Two shoes
Uno/a che tiene un piede in due scarpe
Literally, "someone who keeps one foot in two shoes."

A gossip
Un/a pettegolo/a

A dork
Un secchione
Literally, "a bucket."

A loser
Uno/a sfigato/a
Depending on context, this word gets a lot of mileage; it can also mean "nerd" or "dork."

A wet blanket
Un/a guastafeste

A tool
Un/a imbranato/a

A party pooper
Un/a noiosone/a

A deadbeat
Uno sgarbato

He's got real guts.
*Ha proprio **fegato**.*
Fegato literally means "liver." It's a compliment.

Sorry, but you're not my type.
*Scusami, ma non sei **il mio tipo/la mia tipa**.*

·····Be happy be gay
Sta' bene sta' gay

If you're looking to cruise, you'll find gay and lesbian comunità in the major *città* like Venezia, Milano, Firenze, and Roma with smaller (and harder to find) enclaves outside.

Be discreet: A lot of Italian gays keep things on the down-low, so don't go outing someone by accident. Italian gays, when they're ready, use the same English term "coming out," as well as the Italian *essere allo scoperto* (to be discovered), to describe the process.

Italy's national gay rights organizations Arcigay and Arcilesbica (www.arcigay.it) supported the movement F.U.O.R.I. (whose acronym means "out"). Members supporting the group receive Arcigay Uno membership cards that can be used in participating gay bookstores, clubs, and bars. *Il matrimonio* gay is probably a bit far away for the conservatively minded, mostly Catholic country.

He/She practices…
Lui/Lei pratica…

> **asexuality.**
> *l'asessualità.*
>
> **abstinence.**
> *l'astinenza.*
>
> **heterosexuality.**
> *l'eterosessualità.*
>
> **homosexuality.**
> *l'omosessualità.*
>
> **bisexuality.**
> *la bisessualità.*

He/She is…
Lui/Lei è…

> **straight.**
> *uno/a straight.*
>
> **bi-curious.**
> *bicuriosa.*
>
> **a queer.**
> *una checca.*
> The English word "queer" is also used.
>
> **a gay.**
> *un gay.*

a homosexual.
un omosessuale.

a homo.
un omosex.

a bottom/top.
un/a bottom/top.

a receiver.
un effe.
Literally an "F." This one is pretty offensive.

a queen.
una regina.

an auntie.
una zietta.

a catcher.
un orecchione.
Literally, "big ear." This is very insulting. It's sweeter euphemism is *ricchione*.

a fag.
un finocchio.
Literally, "fennel." This is very offensive.

a faggot.
un frocio.
Also offensive.

a fairy.
un frocetto.

a fruitcake.
uno/a suonato/a nella testa.
This one is pretty offensive, so be careful when using it.

a transgender. (m.)
un transgender.

a transsexual. (m.)
un transessuale.

a transvestite. (m.)
un travestito.

a lesbian.
una lesbica.
The term *saffismo* is also used
to describe lesbianism, from the
Greek lyricist and poet Sappho
(c. 620–570 BC), born on the
island of Lesbos.

a lesbo.
una lesbo.

a dyke.
una lesbicona.

Where can we go cruising?
Dove possiamo fare il battuage?

My favorite color is lavender.
Il mio color preferito è il viola.

Practice safe sex!
Praticate il sesso sicuro!

I practice free love.
Sono praticante del libero amore.

Our relationship is purely platonic.
Il nostro rapporto è completamente platonico.
You did know this term derives from the Greek philosopher
Plato (c. 423–347 BC), didn't you?

I can't stand homophobia.
Non sopporto l'omofobia.

·····My wittle baby-waby
Il mio bimbetto

Whatever your name is in English, the Italians will use the
Italian version. Michael will become Michele, and David will
be Davide, Ann/Anna, Mary/Maria, etc. You can always tell
the Italians are interested by what they call you. Chances
are, they'll quickly assign a *nomino* (pet name) to their
buddies and lovers. It's when their normal speech relaxes

back into the local dialect that the bumpkin talk begins. Do you get me, my little *biscottino*?

With children and good friends, you can add the diminutive *-ino* (or *-ina*) to the end of someone's name (Gabriella becomes Gabriellina, which translates to "Gabby" or "Little Gabby"). Or, you can attach a superlative like *-accio* or *-one* for emphasis (Michele becomes Michelone, which translates to "Big Mike").

Just like in English, where speakers call each other sweetie or honeypie, in Italian you'll hear the old standbys, like *tesoro* (treasure), *angelino* (little angel), and *caro/a* (dear) a thousand times a day in Italy. These monikers are unisex.

Angel
Angelo

Doll
Bambola

Baby doll
Bimba

Beautiful
Bella

Cookie
Biscottino

Dearest
Carissimo/a

Gorgeous
Bellissimo/a

Joy
Gioia

Kitten
Micio

Little one
Piccolino/a

Love
Amore

Lovey
Amorino

Princess
Principessa

Puppy
Cucciolina

Star
Stella

Sugar
Zuccherino

Sweetheart
Dolcezza

·····The art of seduction: sweet talk and begging
L'arte della seduzione: le lusinghe e le suppliche

The caricature of the Italian man pounding his hirsute chest King-Kong style is an insulting, outdated stereotype. Today's typical Italian male is well dressed and stylish, and if he's wearing eyeglasses, they are most certainly designer. What hasn't changed is the fact that an Italian man will do anything to get a woman's attention. He'll tell her she's the most *bella, interessante* woman he's ever met…that he's never felt this way before…that he's been waiting for her *tutta la vita* (his entire life). She may know he's full of shit and will more than likely laugh in his face, but if the *passione* is mutual and *la luna* hits like a big pizza pie, then that's *amore*. So move in bro, and give it your best shot.

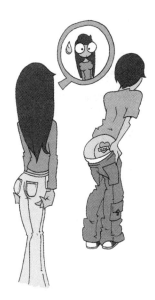

Day and night **I think only of you.**
*Giorno e notte **penso solo a te**.*

Don't tell me your name, **just kiss me.**
*Non dirmi il tuo nome, **baciami e basta**.*

Wanna see my **tattoo?**
*Vuoi vedere il mio **tatuaggio**?*

I'm crazy about you!
***Sono pazzo** di te!*

Without you there's no sun in the sky.
Senza di te non c'è sole in cielo.

You are **my obsession.**
*Sei la **mia ossessione**.*

I can't **think** about anything but you.
*Non faccio altro che **pensare** a te.*

I get lost in your eyes.
***Mi perdo** nei tuoi occhi.*

Marry me or I'll die!
Sposami o morirò!

There's a hole inside me that only you can fill.
C'è un vuoto dentro di me che solo tu puoi colmare.

You are **the most beautiful woman** I've ever seen.
Tu sei la donna più bella che abbia mai visto.

You have stolen my **heart**.
Mi hai rubato il cuore.

You're **the only one**.
Sei l'unica.

Your eyes are like **diamonds**.
I tuoi occhi sono come brillanti.

You have **enchanted** me.
Mi hai incantato/a.

I'm so **horny** for you!
Sono arrapatissimo per te!

Help me, **I'm desperate**!
Aiutami, sono disperato!

I want **to smooch you**.
Voglio pomiciarti.

You have **luscious lips**.
Hai labbra squisite.

If you didn't exist, I'd have to invent you.
Se non ci fossi dovrei inventarti.

You are a **jewel**.
Sei un gioiello.

And if you're hoping to *rimorchiare* (pick up) a cutie, you're wise to avoid saying the wrong thing. Here's *cose da non dire* (what not to say):

You remind me of my ex.
Assomigli a una mia ex.

Can you loan me five bucks/Euros?
Mi puoi prestare cinque dollari/Euro?

Are you also blonde down there?
*Sei **bionda** anche sotto?*

I really like chubby women.
A me piacciono le donne ciccione.

I've got another date in an hour, how's about one for the road?
*Tra un'ora ho un altro appuntamento, ti va una **sveltina**?*

·····Attractive, captivating
Attraente, accattivante

To describe someone obsessed with another person, Italians might say *Fai la bava come le lumache!* (You're foaming like a snail!) Speaking of foam, *mi fa perdere la bava* translates to "she/he makes me drool!" Use these adjectives to describe someone to your BFF.

> **He/She is...**
> *Lui/Lei è...*
>
> > **cool.**
> > *in gamba.*
> >
> > **fun.**
> > *divertente.*
> >
> > **funny.**
> > *buffo/a.*
> >
> > **silly.**
> > *sciocco/a.*
> >
> > **clever.**
> > *furbo/a.*
> >
> > **friendly.**
> > *amichevole*
> >
> > **nice.**
> > *gentile.*

sweet.
dolce.

generous.
generoso/a.

simple.
semplice.

laid-back.
alla mano.

cultured.
colto/a.

spirited.
spiritoso/a.

captivating.
accattivante.

delightful.
delizioso/a.

fascinating.
affascinante.

·····He loves me…he loves me not
Mi ama…non mi ama

It's *l'amore a prima vista*…love at first sight. You're feeling the warm, jittery excitement of new love (just wait…). The endorphins have kicked in and you're over-the-top innamorato (in love). When this happens with an Italian, there is no limit to how totally hokey you can get. Go ahead and gush. Life's too short to hold back.

I love you!
Ti amo!

I love you to death!
Ti amo da morire!

Let's make love.
Facciamo l'amore.

I care about you like no one else.
***Tengo a te** come non tengo a nessun altro.*

If you take my hand, we'll go far.
Prendendomi la mano, noi andremo lontano.
This rhymes in Italian, in case you didn't notice.

I'm sick in love with you!
Ti amo alla follia!

I need you!
Ho bisogno di te!

You are the light in my eyes.
Tu sei la luce dei miei occhi.

I'm enchanted by your stare.
Mi incanto con un tuo sguardo.

You have bewitched me.
Mi hai stregato/a.

You are the man/woman of my dreams!
Sei l'uomo/la donna dei miei sogni!

For you I'd do anything.
Per te farei di tutto.

For love or force.
Per amore o per forza.
Used to describe something inevitable.

You're my whole life.
Sei tutta la mia vita.

You and me forever.
Io e te per sempre.

You're my everything.
Sei il mio tutto.

I hope our story never ends.
Spero che la nostra storia non finisca mai.

CHAPTER 3

PARTY ITALIAN

FESTA ITALIANA

•••••Venues
Locali

You'll find there's no lack of opportunities to party in Italy, whether it's Christmas, New Year's, someone's *compleanno* (birthday), or just *perché* (because). It seems like there are more holidays per year than regular days. And then, of course, there's the old standby "vacation for a day," the *sciopero* (strike), which in Italy is almost always announced beforehand and serves as just another reason to party. As if there weren't enough days to celebrate, Italians also celebrate their *onomastico* (name day), honoring the saint whose name they share. (If your name is Dweezel, you'll probably have to invent your own.)

Do you wanna go out tonight?
Vuoi uscire stasera?

Come on, **let's party!**
Dai, facciamo festa!

☿ COLD BREW NEGRONI

It's not always easy to party long into the night. Adding a little caffeine to that negroni will give you the boost you need to hit the clubs.

GET THESE:

1 ounce gin

1 ounce Campari or Aperol

1½ ounces cold brew coffee

1½ ounces sweet vermouth

orange zest, for garnish

DO THIS:

Fill a large glass with ice cubes and pour in all the ingredients, except for the garnish. Stir until everything is nice and cold, then strain into a rocks glass filled with fresh ice. Squeeze the orange zest over the negroni drink and add it to the glass.

Let's go.
Andiamo.
Andiamo means both "let's go" and "we're going." If the only exposure you've had to the Italian language is through *Dirty Italian*, understanding how to use this verb will help you a lot.

I'm not feeling up for it tonight.
Non mi va per stasera.

Tonight I'm staying home to watch my favorite T.V. show.
Stasera rimango a casa a guardare il mio programmna preferito.

Move your ass. Let's roll.
Alza il culo. Usciamo.

Don't be such a lame-o, come on.
Non essere una palla, dai.

What do you say we go...
Perché non andiamo...

> **dancing.**
> *a ballare.*

> **for a walk.**
> *a fare un giro.*

> **get drunk.**
> *ubriacarci.*

> **have something to drink.**
> *a prendere qualcosa da bere.*

> **listen to music.**
> *ad ascoltare la musica.*

> **watch a movie.**
> *a guardare un film.*

> **see a show.**
> *a vedere uno spettacolo.*

Let's go...
Andiamo...

> **to the club.**
> *in discoteca.*

> **to the pub.**
> *al pub.*

> **to the bar.**
> *al bar.*

> **to that house party you were talking about.**
> *a quella festa di cui parlavi.*

> **anywhere.**
> *dovunque.*

Where's the party at?
Dove sta la festa oggi?

This place is...
Questo posto è...

> **boring.**
> *noioso.*

> **busy.**
> *affollato.*

packed.
pienissimo.

awesome.
grande.
Literally, "big."

crazy.
pazzesca.

off the hook.
in voga.

lame.
palloso.

dead.
morto.

I've got two tickets to a rave.
*Ho due flyer per un rave **party**.*

It's overrated
È uno schianto.

The party was bumping.
***Era pazzesca** la festa.*

What a shithole.
*Che **merdaio**.*

This place is not happening.
Non succeed niente qui.

I've had it. Let's go.
***Sono stufo/a**. Andiamo.*

I can't stay here any longer
Non ci sto più dentro.

·····Drinking
Il bere

Italians hang out in bars from morning till night, but not necessarily to drink themselves into a satisfied stupor. In Italy, *il bar* refers to both a bar and a café. *Il pub* is the best place to go for a *birra*.

If you're an Italian under 25 and still spending money your *mamma* gives you under the *tavolo* (table) because you can't find a job, you'll probably need to rebel (what else is a bored, spoiled kid to do?). Breaking into your parents' liquor cabinet isn't really going to cause a stir given the fact that you've been sipping the fermented juice since your mother first dabbed her finger in wine for your toothless *bocca* (mouth). Nope, if you're a young Italian looking to piss off your parents, you'll drink premixed wine coolers. (It's like traveling to South America, sourcing of some of the world's finest coffee, and seeing everybody go crazy for Nescafé.)

Can I get you something to drink?
*Posso offrirti **qualcosa da bere**?*

How about a glass of wine?
*Ti va un **bicchiere di vino**?*

Red or white?
Rosso o bianco?

CHEERS!)))
CIN CIN!

When Italians *fare un brindisi* (make a toast), they'll say Cin cin (pronounced *cheen cheen*) or *Saluti!* Don't jinx yourself or your hosts by toasting water to wine. Italians are very superstitious about their toasts. If you're not drinking *vino*, just raise your glass but don't clink. In southern Italy there's a tradition in which you must tap the bottom of the wine or beer glass on the top of the table before taking your first sip. Otherwise you're inviting some seriously bad luck to come, and who wants that? Italians never drink without also having something light to nosh on like *patatine* (potato chips) or *noccioline* (peanuts). Saves you from getting embarrassingly drunk. And if you're short on change for real food, you can do a pretty good job filling up on overly salted nibbles.

Can I order a carafe of the house wine?
*Ti va una **caraffa** del vino di casa?*

What do you have on tap?
*Che cosa avete **alla spina**?*

I'll take a bottle of water.
*Prenderò **una bottiglia di acqua**.*
Italian tap water is completely potable, so if you're not into spending three bucks on a bottle of water, just ask for *acqua normale* "normal water."

Chug it! Chug it!
Dai! Bevi!

Why don't we…
Perchè non…

> **take a shot of tequila.**
> *beviamo un **sorso** di tequila.*
>
> **take some shots.**
> *beviamo dei **cicchetti**.*
>
> **order a bottle of prosecco.**
> ***ordinare** una bottigila di prosecco*
>
> **knock back a few.**
> *prendere qualcosa da bere.*

The only thing stupid-ass foreign students want to do is get tanked.
*I maledetti studenti stranieri non vogliono fare altro che **prendersi una sbronza**.*

La birra is also very good in Italy, and if you're over 18 and can't legally drink in the States, welcome to *Italia*!

> **I'll take a cold beer.**
> *Prendo una **birra** fredda.*
>
> **Give me a pint.**
> *Dammi **una pinta**.*
>
> **Do you want some bubbly?**
> *Vuoi **dello spumante**?*

i HAD A HELLUVA OF A TIME)))
MI SONO DIVERTITO/A UNBORDELLO!

After the party is over, Italians love to relive the event by talking about how great it was. You can substitute any of the following. The translations don't work in English so I've given you the literal meaning. All, however, can be used for emphasis.

I had a **helluva** of a time!
*Mi sono divertito/a **un bordello**!*

un bordello (a brothel)

un casino (a whole lot)

una cifra (a fortune)

un fracco (a beating)

un puttanaio (a pile)

un sacco (a sack)

What a shitty beer.
Che birra di merda

This whiskey is totally watered down.
Questo whiskey è completamente annacquato.

•••••Overindulgence
L'eccessiva indulgenza

Italians are no strangers to *eccesso* (excess) and *stravaganza* (extravagance), and the language possesses as many terms for inebriation as there are means to get you there. Tequila and other hard liquors are sometimes referred to as *benzina agricola* (agricultural fuel).

There's a big difference between *bevuto di bello* (happy drunk) and *bevuto di brutto* (stupid drunk), though the transition between the two may be only a couple of glasses of *prosecco*, the Italian equivalent of champagne.

I'm so...
Sono...

That foreign-exchange student is...
Quello studente straniero è...

> **buzzed.**
> *sballato/a.*
>
> **tipsy.**
> *brillo/a.*
>
> **sloshed.**
> *inzuppato/a.*
>
> **drunk.**
> *ubriaco/a.*
>
> **messed up.**
> *massacrato/a.*
>
> **completely shit-faced.**
> *rincoglionito/a.*
>
> **destroyed.**
> *distrutto/a.*
>
> **gone.**
> *andato/a.*
>
> **hammered.**
> *da buttare.*
>
> **out of it.**
> *rovinato/a.*
> Literally, "ruined."
>
> **plastered.**
> *demolito/a.*
> Literally, "demolished."
>
> **smashed.**
> *fatto/a.*
>
> **trashed.**
> *trashato/a.*
>
> **wasted.**
> *sbronzo/a.*
>
> **fucked up.**
> *devastato/a.*
> Literally, "devastated."

Check out that, punk! He's totally smashed.
*Guarda quel punk! Lui è completamente **fatto**.*

The students were wasted off their asses.
*Gli studenti erano **sbronzi fino all'osso**.*
Literally, "drunk to the bone."

Alberto drinks like a fish.
*Alberto beve **come una spugna**.*
Literally, "like a sponge."

You're an alcoholic.
*Sei **alcolizzato/a**.*

·····Smokin'
Il fumo

Believe it or not, *il fumare* (smoking) is now prohibited in most indoor establishments and public spaces like airports in Italy. Tobacco can be purchased at the *tabaccheria* (tobacco shop) and many bars. A minority of Italians smoke a combination of hash (or weed) and tobacco. A *purino* is pure reefer and is rarely smoked. That being said, *fuma bene, fuma sano, fuma sempre pakistano* (smoke well, smoke healthy, always smoke Pakistan).

Do you smoke?
Fumi?

Can I bum a smoke?
*Posso fregarti una **siga**?*

Do you have a light?
*Hai d'**accendere**?*

Do you have rolling papers?
*Hai un **papier**?*

Is it okay if I smoke a cigarette?
*Va bene se fumo una **sigaretta**?*

Light me up!
Fammi accendere!

Mind if I light up a joint?
Mi faccio una canna?

·····Drugs
La droga

Italian laws are damn harsh when it comes to illegal drugs whether you're talking about cocaine, heroin, hashish, or marijuana. Even recreational use is considered excessive. I don't know about you, but I'd have a glass of *vino* instead. There are certainly better places to spend my time than inside an Italian *prigione* (prison).

Blow
La bomba
Literally, "bomb."

Cocaine
La cocaina

Coke
La coca

Ecstasy pills
Le pasticchette di ecstasy

Ganja
La gangia

Grass
Il basilico
Literally, "basil."

Herb
L'erba

Marijuana
La marijuana

Maryjane
La Maria

Pot
La roba

A doobie
Un flower

A hit
Un tiro

> Go on, **take a hit.**
> *Dai, **tira**.*

A joint
Una canna

A line
Un colpo
Literally, "hit."

A spliff
Una fiamma
Literally, "flame."

A stick
Uno spinello

A twist
Una paglia
Literally, "straw," like hay…not the kind you snort with.

Give me a pill.
*Dammi una **pasta**.*
The word *pasta* in this case refers to any mind-altering pill such as ecstasy. Also used are the words *pasticca, chicca,* and *trip.*

He's such a chain-smoking pothead.
Quello ha fumato l'ombra di un bosco.
Literally, "He smoked the shadow of a forest."

He/She is…
Lui/lei è…

> high.
> *fuori.*
> Literally, "out."

so high.
fuori duro.

toasted.
stravolto/a.

blazed.
allegro/a.

baked.
ciuccio/a.

faded.
spento come un fiammifero.
Literally, "out like a match."

ripped.
schizzato/a.

tweaking.
in paranoia.

stoned.
fumato/a.

tripping out.
pasticcato/a.

a drug addict.
un tossicodipendente.

a junkie.
un tossico.

·····Hungover
Sbronzo

The Italians and their ancestors have been partying for a long time, actually since around 200 BC. The *bacchanalia* were the ecstatic, mystical festivals based on the Bacchus cult. Nothing short of an unruly frat party, drinking games included sucking down as many cups of wine as indicated by the throw of the dice. Contrary to popular thinking, the Romans did not have separate vomit rooms for this purpose. Like a bunch of wet-eared freshmen, they just found the closest toilet and let it all out in time for the next round, but there were also special bowls placed near tables for the same reason.

Amazingly, Italian does not have a precise term for "hangover." You can say *il dopo-sbornia* (the after plaster) and *doposbronzo*, but these still aren't quite the same as the English (which is not to say Italians don't get hungover).

Dude, is everything okay?
Amico, tutto okay?

I drank way to much last night.
***Ho bevuto** troppo ieri notte.*

I feel like **shit.**
*Mi sento come la **merda**.*

I'm so **hungover.**
*Sono proprio **sbronzo/a**.*

I got totally plastered last night.
***Mi sono preso una bella sbornia** ieri notte.*

Do you have any aspirin? I've got a killer **headache.**
*Hai della aspirina? Ho un brutto **mal di testa**.*

My head is about to **explode.**
*La testa sta per **esplodere**.*

I'm nauseous.
Mi sento la nausea.

I have the spins.
Mi gira la testa.

He vomited all night.
Ha vomitato tutta la notte.

I threw up in my bed last night.
Ieri notte ho rigettato a letto.

·····Cops
La pula

You can easily spot the *carabinieri*, Italy's military police, not to be confused with the local *polizia* (police). They're the uniformed studs you see in airports and *stazioni* with big guns slung over their shoulders. Their job, aside from protecting the country from *terroristi*, is to scare the *crapola* out of you. They're not like the friendly, fuzzy-headed, Buckingham Palace guards who won't even blink if you crap on their shoes. That said, most *carabinieri* are still going home to *mamma* when the day is done.

The police are coming!
Arriva la polizia!

Coppers
I caramba

Fuzz
Gli sbirri

Pigs
I piedipiatti
Literally, "flatfoots."

Police officer
Il poliziotto/la poliziotta

KNOCK KNOCK!)))
BUSSA BUSSA!

The *carabinieri* are the butt of many a joke. Here's are a couple to impress your friends.

How many carabinieri does it take to screw in a light bulb?
Quanti carabinieri servono per avvitare una lampadina?

One thousand and one: One to hold the light bulb and a thousand to screw the building.
Mille e uno: Uno tiene ferma la lampadina e mille l'avvitano.

"Heaven is where the police are British, the chefs are French, the mechanics are German, the lovers Italian, and it's all organized by the Swiss. Hell is where the chefs are British, the mechanics are French, the lovers are Swiss, the police are German, and it's all organized by the Italians."

Po-po
Lo sgherro

Traffic cop
Il vigile/la vigilessa

CHAPTER 4

BODY ITALIAN
IL CORPO ITALIANO

Italians have a funny habit of *fissando lo sguardo* (staring each other down) when they're out walking. Unlike North Americans and northern Europeans, they feel no *compulsione* to acknowledge the fact that you exist. Without apology, they'll scan you *dalla testa ai piedi* (from head to toe). Chances are you've been assessed, dissed, and dismissed before the scent of their cologne or *profumo* (perfume) has even caught up with you. *La soluzione*: Learn how to stare back. Not with those beady eyes—the stare should be unapologetic, piercing, and deadpan, no emotions attached.

·····Nice body!
che corpo!

You are...
Tu sei...

He/She is...
Lui/Lei è...

> **cute.**
> *carino/a.*

ITALIAN OLD-FASHIONED

Beer goggles are one thing. Bourbon goggles are quite another. Everyone looks *bellissimo* after you've had a few of these.

GET THESE:

    3 ounces bourbon

    ½ ounce Luxardo liqueur

    ¾ ounce Crème de Cocoa liqueur

    2 dashes chocolate bitters

    1 dash cherry bitters

    cocktail cherry, for garnish

DO THIS:

Add the first five ingredients to a cocktail shaker with ice. Shake until the cocktail is well chilled and strain it into your prettiest rocks glass filled with fresh ice, then garnish with a cocktail cherry.

attractive.
attraente.

beautiful.
bello/a.

fine.
togo/a.

gorgeous.
bellissimo/a.

boyish/girlish.
fanciullesco/a.

in shape.
in forma.

muscular.
muscoloso/a.

bangin'.
provocante.

sexy.
sexy.

stylish.
di moda.

Your GF is a total…
La tua ragazza è veramente una…

> **babe!**
> *bona!*

> **bombshell!**
> *bella strada di montagna!*
> Literally, "a nice mountain road," referring to a woman
> with curves.

> **knock-out!**
> *sventola!*
> Literally, "a slap."

> **MILF!**
> *mamma da scopare*

> **real woman!**
> *vera donna!*

> **well-built woman!**
> *maggiorata!*

Man! He is such…
Caspita! Lui è proprio…

> **a dream!**
> *un incanto!*

> **a babe!**
> *uno bono!*

a hunk!
un fusto!

a real man!
un uomo vero!

a stud!
un fichetto
From the word fico.

She is smokin' hot!
Lei è fighissima!

**According to People magazine, Bradley Cooper is
one of the sexiest men in the world.**
*Secondo la rivista People, Bradley Cooper è uno degli
uomini più sexy del mondo.*

I want a man who is tall, dark, and handsome.
Voglio un uomo bel tenebroso.

He's/She's got...
Lui/Lei ha...

> **a nice body.**
> *un bel corpo.*
>
> **a hot bod.**
> *un corpo provocante.*
>
> **an attractive look.**
> *un bell'aspetto.*
>
> **a body to die for.**
> *un fisico niente male.*
>
> **a really cute belly button.**
> *un ombelico molto carino.*
>
> **killer legs.**
> *le gambe da morire.*

·····Ugly as sin
Brutto come un peccato

Not everyone is a walking version of *Venere* (Venus) or
Marte (Mars).

Hot damn! You are…
Ammazza! Sei…

If you ask me, he's/she's…
Secondo me, è…

> **kinda funny looking.**
> *un po' strano/a.*
>
> **heinous.**
> *bruttissimo/a.*
>
> **chubby.**
> *ciccio/a (also ciccione).*
>
> **fat.**
> *grossaccio/a.*
>
> **hairy.**
> *peloso/a.*
>
> **bald.**
> *calvo/a.*
>
> **bug-eyed.**
> *occhi a palla.*
> Literally, "eyes of a ball."
>
> **gap-toothed.**
> *sdentato/a.*
>
> **smelly.**
> *puzzolente.*
>
> **fugly.**
> *brutto/a come il demonio.*
> Literally, "ugly as a demon."
>
> **pitiful.**
> *brutto/a come il diavolo,*
> Literally, "ugly as the devil."
>
> **nasty.**
> *brutto/a come la fame.*
> Literally, "ugly as hunger."
>
> **ugly as a toad.**
> *brutto/a come un rospo.*
>
> **ugly as sin.**
> *brutto/a come il peccato.*

Her/his good looks are only skin deep.
Ha la bellezza dell'asino.
Literally, "She/he's got beauty of an ass." The donkey refers to someone whose good looks are the result of being young.

You're so fat that wherever I look, you're already there!
*Sei talmente **grasso/a** che ovunque guardo stai già là!*

Your sister is so ugly that if she tried to become a whore, she'd have to pay the clients.
*Tua sorella è così **brutta** che se va a fare la **puttana**, è lei che deve pagare i clienti.*

·····You're too skinny!
Sei troppo magra!

It's an understatement to say that Italians are comfortable talking about their bodies. Maybe they just like making Brits and Americans blush, but there's hardly anything regarding the body that Italians won't discuss. And if you think everyone is so *svelte* because they walk twenty miles a day, think again. Italians (especially of the female persuasion) are as obsessed with *dimagrire/ingrassare* (losing weight/ gaining weight) as Americans are. A typical *complimento* to a friend is to ask if she recently lost weight. A double compliment to say that someone has really gone too far.

Skinny
Magro/a

Scrawny
Pelle e ossa
Literally, "skin and bones."

I've gained weight.
*Sono **ingrassato/a**.*

No you haven't, you've lost weight.
*Non è vero, **sei dimagrito/a**.*

SUPER HOT!)))
FICHISSIMO!

It's worth mentioning that *un fico* isn't just a fig. Also pronounced *figo*, the term refers to a very attractive Italian male, the kind that makes you suck in your breath and start shakin' your hand up and down. There are a few variations used along this theme for both sexes.

For Him

> a hottie
> *un fico/figo*
>
> a major hottie
> *un ficone*
>
> hella hot
> *strafico/strafigo*
>
> Johnny Depp is **hella hot**.
> *Johnny Depp è **strafico/strafigo**.*
>
> crazy hot
> *fichissimo*
>
>> Yeah, but [insert your favorite fantasia] is **crazy hot**.
>> *Sì, ma [_____] è **fichissimo**.*

For Her

The general terms *fica* and *figa* are used to describe a really hot chick. But wait a hot second before you start flinging these words around someone's daughter. Remember that *fica* also refers to a woman's genitalia, so use it with caution. Better yet, avoid using *fica* altogether.

> a hottie
> *una figa*
>
> a super hottie
> *una figa spaziale*
>
> hella hot
> *strafiga*
>
>> Scarlett Johansson is **hella hot**.
>> *Scarlett Johansson è **strafiga**.*
>
> insane hot
> *fichissima*
>
>> No doubt, but Penelope Cruz is **insane hot**.
>> *Senza dubbio, ma Penelope Cruz è **fichisima**.*

Don't overdo it now!
Non esagerare!

You're skinny as a rail!
Sei magro/a come un chiodo!
Literally, "skinny as a nail."

You're such a liar.
Sei proprio un bugiardo/a.

I wouldn't lie to you.
Non ti mentirei.

·····Boobs
Le bocce

Boobies, tits, melons, pebbles—just like in English, Italian has tons of euphemisms for breasts. The most common terms are *il seno* (breast) and *le tette* (tits). *Ce l'ha sode* refers to a well-endowed woman.

Can I touch your…?
Posso toccare…?

Do you want to touch my…?
Vuoi toccare…?

> **bust**
> *il petto*
>
> **hooters**
> *le poppe*
>
> **breasts**
> *il seno*
>
> **tits**
> *le tette*
>
> **rack**
> *il balcone*
> Literally, "balcony."
>
> **milk cans**
> *le colombe*
> Literally, "doves."

mams
le mammelle

jugs
le melanzane
Literally, "eggplants."

melons
i meloni

Dina isn't fat; she's stacked.
Dina non è grassa; è una maggiorata.

Check out those tits!
Guarda che tette!

Wow, what a huge rack!
Mamma mia, che tette enormi!

Maria is flat chested, but she's really sexy.
Maria ha poco seno, ma è molto sexy.

She has nipples like saucers.
Ha i capezzoli come piattini.

Did you see that big-titted fatty in the pool?
Hai visto quella tettona grassa nella piscina?

Pamela Anderson has round and firm breasts.
Pamela Anderson ha i seni rotondi e sodi.

But they're not real.
Ma non sono veri.

·····Ass
Il culo

Whether you're talking about an ass, butt, bum, or badonkadonk, the most commonly heard term is *culo*. Add *-ne* and you have *culone* (big ass), some serious junk in the trunk. A sexy girl with a beautiful derriere would be described as *una bellesponde* (beautiful banks).

Tush
Il dedrio

Tail
Il posteriore

Butt
Il fracco

Caboose
Il fiocco
Literally, "bow."

Cheeks
I fondelli ; Le chiappe

Heinie
Il mazzo
Literally, "cluster."

Rear end
Il contrabbasso
Literally, "contrabase."

Rump
Il melone
Literally, "melon."

Apple bottom
Le mele

Bubble butt
Il balconcino
Literally, "balcony."

Big ass
Il culone

Badonkadonk
Il cannone
Literally, "canon."

Cushion
Il pallone
Literally, "big ball."

Booty
Canestro

ASS SPEAK)))
IL LINGUAGGIO DEL CULO

Il culo (ass) is a word used in a gazillion ways. The end piece of a loaf of bread or a block of cheese is called a *culo*, whereas *una culata* is a bump made with one's backside (do the humpty hump).

There are a few ass-related *espressioni* worth holding on to. *Un dito in culo* (a finger in the ass) is a pain in the ass. If someone lives in *culo al mondo* (in the ass of the world) it means they live in the boonies. *Non ha freddo nel culo* (he doesn't have a cold ass) refers to someone who's flush with cash.

Che culo hai!
You're one lucky S.O.B.
Literally, "to have ass."

Mario is a total **ass kisser**.
*Mario è **propio un leccaculo**.*

You're **shameless as an ass**.
*Hai la **faccia peggio del culo**.*

Phineas and Ferb are **thick as thieves**.
*Phineas e Ferb sono **culo e camicia**.*
Literally, "to be ass and shirt with someone."

I busted my ass finding you ice cream at this hour.
***Mi sono fatto il culo** per trovarti il gelato a quest'ora.*

The project **went to shit**.
*Il progetto è **andato in culo**.*
Literally, "to go to the ass."

It seems like **she's/he's got eyes in the back of his/her head**.
*Sembra che **abbia gli occhi anche nel culo**.*
Literally, "to have eyes up your ass."

Are you **jerking me around**?
*Mi stai **prendendo per il culo**?*
Literally, "to catch by the ass."

Get your ass in gear; we're late!
***Alza il culo**; siamo in ritardo!*

What a **stroke** of luck!
*Che **botta** di culo!*
Literally, "What a hit of ass!"; *butta di culo* is also used.

COMFORTS)))
I CONFORTI

In the old days, public toilets were nothing more than a drain hole in the middle of a generally filthy tiled room, often without a door. *Che puzzo!* (What a stink!) These days, most public restrooms have a standard toilet so you don't need to get your fingers all germy. In case they need to drop the kids off at the pool, Italians on-the-go keep some extra change handy to plug into the turnstile at the public restrooms found in bus and train terminals. (McDonald's is also a great pit stop).

bathroom	*il bagno*
bidet	*il bidè*
commode	*la latrina*
crapper	*il cesso*
pisser	*il pisciatoio*
shitter	*il gabinetto*
throne	*il trono*
John	*la toilette*
toilet seat	*il trono* (throne)
urinal	*il vespasiano*

Trunk
La tasca
Literally, "pocket."

•••••Clean fun
Il divertimento pulito

When in a bather's paradise like Italy, do as the bathers do and steep yourself in one of the many *terme* (thermal baths) located throughout the country. There's no better way to check out the goods without seeming too obvious (pervert!). In the old days, you could go to *i bagni* (the bathhouses) to find all sorts of lustful pleasures. The *bagni di gruppo* (group baths) were popular among adulterous high-ranking men to get a little bunga-bunga on the side.

BTW, feel free to soak up until you get pruney in these bathhouses, but know that it's not so cool to take hour-long showers like you do back home. You'll use up all the *acqua calda* (hot water), you vulgar, oblivious, energy hog!

Let's go chill at the spa.
*Andiamo a rilassarci al **centro benessere***.
Literally, "well-being center."

The water's hella hot/freezing.
*L'acqua è **bollente/ghiacciata***.

I'd like...
Vorrei...

> **a nice massage.**
> *un bel massaggio.*
>
> **a manicure.**
> *una manicure.*
>
> **a pedicure.**
> *una pedicure.*
>
> **a facial.**
> *un facciale.*
>
> **a mud bath.**
> *un bagno di fango.*
>
> **a blow job.**
> *un pompino.*
>
> **a bathrobe.**
> *un accappatoio.*

·····Pissing and shitting
Il pisciare e il cagare

You may think you're hysterical playing "pull my finger," but some things are best kept private. The next time you bust ass, step on a duck, or cut a muffin, blame it on the dog.

Where's the can?
Dov'è il cesso?

I gotta...
Devo..

>   **go to the bathroom.**
>   *andare in bagno.*
>
>   **go pee.**
>   *fare la pipì.*
>
>   **take a piss.**
>   *fare una pisciata.*
>
>   **piss.**
>   *pisciare.*
>
>   **crap.**
>   *cagare.*
>
>   **take a crap.**
>   *fare una cagata.*

I laughed so hard I pissed myself.
***Mi sono pisciato addosso** dalle risate.*

Poop
Cacca

Excrement
L'escremento

Feces
Le feci

Droppings
Lo sterco

Poo-poo
La popò

Doodie
Il pupù

A little turd
Una caccola

Shit
La merda

Diarrhea
La cacarella

There's nothing like a good crap.
*Non c'è niente come una bella **cagata**.*

I have the runs.
*Ho **la cagarella**.*

I'm constipated.
Sono stitico/a.

•••••Other bodily functions
Le altre funzioni corporei

Just burp it out.
*Fatti un bel **rutto**.*

I've got the hiccups.
*Ho il **singhiozzo**.*

A fart
Una scoreggia
It's no wonder they call those loud motorcycles *scorreggioni* (big farts).

BEAUTIFUL SHIT)))
BELL A MERDA

You're shit in luck because the Italians use the word *merda* pretty much the same way English speakers use the word "shit." In addition, there are quite a few similar expressions related to scat. *Un pezzo di merda* refers to "a piece of shit," and *un sacco di merda* refers to "a sack of shit."

Particularly useful when you bang your thumb with a hammer is *Merda per merda!* (Shit for shit!)

Enrico is a **shitface**.
*Enrico ha una **faccia di merda**.*

What a **shitty** film!
*Che film **di merda**!*

I'm **up to my neck** in shit.
*Sono proprio nella merda **fino al collo**!*

You're a real **shit**.
*Sei proprio una **merda**.*

What a **shithead**!
*Che **Testa di merda**!*

What a **shithole**.
*Che **merdaio**.*

You make a **shitty impression** when you act like an turd.
*Fai una **figura di merda** quando ti comporti come uno stronzo.*

You're in deep shit!
Sei nella merda!

Eat shit and die!
***Mangia merda** e muore!*

Enjoy these shitty *proverbi* (proverbs):

Running and shitting you'll get shit all over yourself.
*A **correre e cagare** ci si immerda i garretti.*
Used when you're trying to do too much at once.

If March throws out grass, April **throws shit**.
*Se marzo butta erba, aprile **butta merda**.*
The pessimistic version of "April showers bring May flowers."

Who's the nasty-ass that farted?
Quale di voi bestie ha scoreggiato?

It wasn't me who cut the cheese.
Non ero io a fare quel puzzo.
Literally, "made a stink."

Who ripped one?
Chi ha fatto quel peto?

Ladies don't fart, they poot.
Le donne non scoreggiano, fanno aria.
Literally, "make air."

Ewww…smegma!
Ewww…smegma!

He totally eats his boogers, I've seen it.
Lui mangia il moccio, l'ho visto.

You have bad breath! What'd ya eat, a dead baby?
Ha l'alito pesante! Cos'hai mangiato, un bambino morto?

You smell like a goat after three days in the sun.
Puzzi come una capra dopo tre giorni al sole.

That's a helluva…
Mamma, che…

> **pimple.**
> *brufolo.*

> **black head.**
> *punto nero.*

> **volcano.**
> *vulcano.*

> **zit.**
> *puntina.*

To squeeze or not to squeeze?
Schiacciare o non schiacciare?

Quit playing with it.
Lascialo.

·····I don't feel so good
Mi sento male

Italy is a hypochondriac's heaven. If you're looking for attention in Italy, nothing works better than playing the old sick card. Italians, in addition to blaming a lot on the *fegato* (liver), are also obsessed with *la digestione* (digestion) and making sure they don't catch *un colpo d'aria* (a draft). Italians will never:

Go swimming for at least two hours after eating This could seriously *bloccare la digestione* (block your digestion). An ill-timed *cappuccino* (especially after a meal) can also affect your *digestione*.

Open a window in a train or anywhere *Un colpo d'aria* might somehow manage to seep in and cause countless problems including chills, stiff necks, and sore backs.

Get caught in the rain without an *ombrello* (umbrella) God forbid they should get their hair wet—it could lead to any number of chronic illnesses including *la cervicale* (cervical arthrosis), a particularly common ailment in Italy whose symptoms include nausea, neck stiffness, and *mal di testa* (headache).

Are you all right?
Va tutto bene?

Are you sick?
Stai male?

Call a doctor!
Chiama il medico!

Get me an aspirin.
Dammi un'aspirina.

I can't work today…
Non posso lavorare oggi…

I'm sick.
sto male.

I have my period.
*mi sono venute le **mestruazioni**.*

I'm on the rag.
*ho le **mie cose**.*
Literally, "I have my thing."

I've got a bad liver.
*ho **mal di fegato**.*

I caught a draft.
*mi sono preso/a **un colpo d'aria**.*

I caught a cold.
*ho il **raffredore**.*

I don't feel well.
*non **mi sento bene**.*

I feel bad.
mi sento male.

I feel like shit.
sto di merda.

I have a sore throat.
*ho **mal di gola**.*

I think I'm gonna vomit.
sto per vomitare.

I'm bleeding.
sto perdendo sangue.

I feel itchy.
mi sento il prurito.

my belly hurts.
*mi fa male la **pancia**.*

Not now…I've got a headache.
*Non ora, ho un **mal di testa**.*

The cold gives me goosebumps.
*Il freddo mi dà la **pelle d'oca**.*

I'm not well today because I have cervicale.
Oggi non sto bene perché ho la cervicale.

CHAPTER 5

HORNY ITALIAN
ITALIANO ARRAPATO

Let's face it, if you're here for the bunga-bunga then *vergognati!* (shame on you!) If it's any consolation, you're in good company. To the Italians, sex isn't only about pleasure or making babies; it's a cure-all for everything from dry skin to back pain to menstrual cramps. *Il sesso* is a natural part of life, and enjoying its variances is vital to maintaining a state of *benessere* (well-being).

·····Fucking
Lo scopare

I wanna…
Vorrei…

> **bang.**
> *dare dei colpi.*
>
> **beat.**
> *sbattere.*
>
> **mount you.**
> *montarti.*
>
> **penetrate.**
> *penetrare.*

BUNGA BUNGA

Naughty sex isn't just for prime ministers anymore.

GET THESE:

1 ounce fresh lime juice

1 teaspoon white sugar

8 mint leaves

handful of fresh blueberries

2 ounces white rum

1 ounce club soda

lime wedge, for garnish

DO THIS:

Add the lime juice, sugar, mint, and blueberries to a rocks glass and muddle until the sugar is dissolved. Add the rum, stir well, and then fill the glass with ice. Top with a little club soda to make the drink a little bubbly. Garnish with a lime wedge. Sip and get in the mood.

screw.
chiavare.
Literally, "to key."

play the contrabass.
suonare il contrabasso.

play the trumpet.
trombare.

plow.
arare.

screw.
fottere.

shag.
ciulare.

de-virginize someone.
sverginare qualcuno/a.

·····Positions
Le posizioni

Italians understand that variety is the spice of life. Although making love is a universal language, there are a couple of Italian terms worth noting. For instance, instead of doing it "doggy-style," the Italians do it *alla pecorina* (sheep-style). *L'amazzone* (the Amazonian) is the term used to describe when a woman sits on a man's face. (It's also called *la pompeiana* given the position was first depicted on frescoes in Pompeii.) The *sultano* (sultan) describes when a man gets blown by a woman who is crouched between his thighs. Naturally, there are far more variations and regional terms than those listed here.

Do you wanna change positions?
Vuoi voltare il disco?
Literally, "to turn the record over."

SƏXUAL RAPPORT)))
IL RAPPORTO SESSUALE

The Italian word *scopa* has a bunch of meanings: The Italians love to play a card game called *scopa*, and *una scopa* is a broom; change the noun to masculine and it becomes *lo scopo* (the goal). *Scopare* is a verb that literally means "to sweep," but in street speak means "to fuck," so next time you sweep the floor—unless it's on all fours— avoid using *scopare*. Most of you reading this wouldn't be old enough to have seen Lena Wertmuller's film *Swept Away*, but when you do finally get the chance, now you'll get the double *entendre*.

Let's have **a good fuck**!
*Ci vuole **una bella scopata**!*

We fucked a couple of times.
***Ci siamo scopati** un paio di volte.*

Do you wanna **shag** in the car?
*Vuoi **trombare** in macchina?*

What are you in the mood for?
Come ti va?

What's your preference?
Qual è la tua preferenza?

I like…
Mi piace…

How 'bout…?
Come va…?

> **the missionary position**
> *la posizione del missionario*

> **woman on top**
> *la donna sopra*

> **the cowgirl**
> *la smorzacandela*
> Literally, "the candle snuffer."

> **sixty-nine**
> *il sessantanove*

> **doggy-style**
> *la posizione alla pecorina*
> Literally, "sheep style."

> **through the back door**
> *da dietro*

> **the wheelbarrow**
> *la carriola*

> **a ménage a trois**
> *un ménage a trios*

> **a threesome**
> *un triangolo*
> Literally, "triangle."

Do you wanna…?
Vuoi…?

> **give me a rim job**
> *farmi l'anilingus*

> **fuck in the ass**
> *buggerare*

TO SWITCH)))
FARE LO SWITCH

> Him: Whadda ya' say, should **we change positions** this evening?
> *Lui: Che ne dici, **cambiamo posizioni stasera**?*
>
> Her: Great idea! You get dinner ready, while I'll sit on the couch and fart.
> *Lei: Ottima idea! Tu prepari la cena, mentre io mi siedo sul divano e scorreggio!*

titty-fuck
fare una spagnola
Literally, "do the Spanish thing."

have anal sex
inculare
Also used to describe when someone has been ripped off or "fucked over."

take it from the behind
suonare il tamburo
Literally, "to play the drum."

I prefer a nice erotic massage as foreplay.
*Preferisco un bel massaggio erotico come **preliminare**.*

·····The act
L'atto

It's not a race, so *pazienza*. Italians know it's the journey that counts, not the destination.

Let's have an adventure/an affair.
*Facciamo un'**avventura/una storia**.*

Is there somewhere more private we can go?
*C'e una parte più **privata** dove si può stare?*

Do you want to come to my place?
*Vuoi venire **a casa mia**?*

Tell me how you like it.
*Dimmi come **ti piace**.*

What's your fantasy?
*Qual è la tua **fantasia**?*

I'm starving for you!
Sono allupato/a per te!

I'm so horny for you!
*Sono proprio **arrapato/a** per te!*

I'm ready for you.
Sono pronto/a per te.

You turn me on!
M'attizzi!

Get undressed.
Spogliati.

Lay down.
Sdraiati.

Bend over.
Chinati.

Tell me that you're my slut.
*Dimmi che sei la **mia troia**.*

Hurry!
Sbrigati!

Go slow.
Piano piano.

Come on, touch it!
Dai, tocca ferro!

Give it to me.
Dammelo.

KiSSiNG)))
IL BACIARE

Ever loyal to their *madrelingua* (native tongue), instead of French kissing, Italians simply *baciare* con *la lingua* (to kiss with the tongue). *Una slinguata* (tongue job) derives from the word *lingua* (tongue), the same root from which we get that wonderful word "cunnilingus." Give it up for the cunning linguist!

Kiss me!
Baciami!

We French kissed.
Ci siamo baciati con la lingua.

Come on, give me **a kiss**!
*Dai, dammi **un bacio**!*

Did you **make-out**?
*Ci sei **andato/a**?*

Did you **go all the way**?
*Ma, ci sei **andato andato**?*

Who gave you that **hickey**?
*Chi ti ha dato quel **succhiotto**?*

We tongued each other for two hours.
***Ci siamo slinguati** per due ore.*

I'm excited.
Mi sono eccitato/a.

Put it in your mouth.
Prendilo in bocca.

I'll give you anything you want.
Ti darò qualsiasi cosa che desideri.

Oh, yeah.
Ah sì.

That's the spot.
Così va bene.

Don't stop!
Non smettere!

I'm about to come!
Sto per venire!

I'm coming!
Vengo! ; Arrivo!

He was so excited he blew his load.
Era così eccitato che si è bagnato addosso.

I exploded with pleasure.
Sono scoppiato/a dal piacere.

Sweet dreams!
Sogni d'oro!

You can go away now.
Ora, puoi andare via.

·····Wanna have a quickie?
Facciamo una sveltina?

It could be between *amanti* or a chance encounter; in either case, *una sveltina* generally does not require getting undressed (beyond what's necessary). And don't expect to cuddle afterward.

We had a quickie in between appointments.
Ci siamo fatti una sveltina tra gli appuntamenti.
You can also use the Americanized version, *un quiko*.

We had a nooner during lunch break.
Abbiamo fatto una scopatina durante l'ora di pranzo.
Scopatina can also be used for "quickie."

We don't have much time. Let's make it fast.
Non abbiamo molto tempo. Facciamo una cosina veloce.
Literally, "to have a fast little thing."

Let's do it in the car.
Facciamo il sesso a quattro ruote.
For the Italians, *il sesso a quattro ruote* (sex on four wheels)
is like spaghetti, soccer, and good wine, especially since
the invention of the adjustable seat. In a survey of 18 to 24
year olds taken among eight European countries, Italians
indicated the car as their favorite place to fool around.
One of the other more practical reasons for this is that
most Italians live with their parents until they're in their late
thirties or they share housing, so the only place they can
do it is in the car. To avoid more trouble than it's worth,
make sure you park in a discreet place, cover the windows
with newspaper (don't forget the tape), and for godsakes,
please lock the doors.

We schtuped in the car. My back aches.
*Abbiamo fatto una trombata in macchina. Mi fa male la
schiena.*

•••••Penis love
L'Amore del pene

The ancient Romans practically worshipped the cock.
They made it into a religion and backed it up with lots of
juicy images of thrusting pagans alongside enormous

depictions of the male member. The frescoes preserved in Pompeii and other Roman hot spots are proof that the love affair Italian men have with their sausages ain't nothin' new. The Latin phrase *Hic Habitat Felicitas* said it all: Here Lies Happiness. You won't find a lot of argument there.

She just wants my...
Vuole solo il mio...

> **dick.**
> *cazzo.*

> **tireless cock.**
> *spada instancabile.*

> **willy.**
> *pipì.*

> **member.**
> *membro.*

> **donkey dick.**
> *superdotato.*
> Otherwise known as well-endowed.

TOOLS)))
ARNESI

Hey stud, wave your *bastone* (magic wand) over here!

> club
> *mazza*

> flagpole
> *bandeira*

> handle
> *manico*

> rod
> *verga*

> screwdriver
> *cacciavite*

schlong!
minchia!
Although it has come to singularly mean "dick," the Sicilian term for penis derives from the Latin *mentula*, meaning "stalk" or "tail." It's heard mostly in southern dialects including Calabrese, Barese, and Sicilian, and now *Minchia*! is also used to say "Fuck!" or "Shit!"

phallus.
fallo.

foreskin.
il prepuzio.

hood.
cappuccio.
Also used to refer to a condom.

His flag is at **half-mast.**
*Ha la bandiera a **mezz'asta**.*
Basically, "dude's got a limp dick."

Girth is more important than length.
Bello, grande, grosso.
Literally, "beautiful, big, thick."

Do you know where I can score some Viagra?
Sa dove posso trovare il Viagra?

I want to...
Voglio...

    dip the stick.
    inzuppare il biscotto.
    Literally, "to dip the cookie."

    play the skin flute.
    suonare il flauto a pelle.

    put the horse in the stable.
    mettere il cavallo nella stalla.

    suck your lollipop.
    succhiare il tuo lecca lecca.

Tell me if you've ever seen a dick this big.
*Dimmi che non hai mai visto **un cazzo così grande**.*

LOLLIPOP-LOLLIPOP)))
LECCA-LECCA

When it comes to describing everyone's favorite body parts, Italian and English have more than a few words in common. For example, *banana* (banana), *carota* (carrot), and *spada* (sword) are all used to describe dicks. Likewise, the Italian words for *caverna* (cavern), *pelo* (fur), *fessa* (crack), and *Giovannina* (Ginny) all describe pussy.

On the other hand, it can be confusing when both languages utilize the same word to describe different things. Take the word *susina* (plum): While in English it can refer to a man's testicle, in Italian it can also mean a pussy. In English, the word "cookie" can also imply a pussy, but in Italian the word *biscotto* describes a Johnson. (By the way, it's pronounced *bees-KOHT-toh*, and not "biscotty" that rhymes with "potty.")

banana
banana
Or *ciquita*, like the brand name.

twinky
biscotto

carrot
carota

chode
fava
Literally, "fava bean."

pisser
pisello
Literally, "pea."

prick
cactus
Like the prickly desert plant.

sausage
salsiccia

wang
asparago
Literally, "asparagus."

winkle
pisellino
Literally, "little pee."

What a...dick you have.
Che cazzo...hai!

> **small / tiny**
> *piccolo / piccolissimo*

> **big / huge**
> *grande / grandissimo*

> **hard**
> *duro*

> **flaccid**
> *flaccido*

ANiMALS)))
ANIMALI

Aside from *uccello* (bird), most of the animal terms used to describe cocks aren't exactly flattering.

> **cockroach**
> *bagarozzo*

> **canary**
> *canarino*
> Used for a small penis.

> **Limp dick**
> *baccalà*
> Literally, "dried codfish."

> **maggot**
> *verme*
> Refers to a small penis.

> **pecker**
> *uccello*
> Literally, "bird."

> **worm**
> *baco*

> **fish**
> *pesce*

> **eel**
> *anguilla*

well-endowed
superdotato

long / really long
lungo / lunghissimo

thick / really thick
grosso / grossissimo

I have…
Ho…

a hard-on.
un cazzo duro.

a pump.
una pompa.

a joy boner.
un cazzo dritto.
Literally, "a straight dick."

I've got a woody.
Sono a **mezzogiorno**.
Literally, "I'm at noon."

Are you circumcised?
Ti hanno **fatto la circoncisione**?

·····Sword swallowing
L'arte Bolognese

L'arte Bolognese refers to the art of sword swallowing. The following terms are particularly dirty, lacking class, and overall *sgarbo* (crude) and *maleducato* (rude).

Do you like to give head?
Ti piace **fare il pompino**?

Come here and sit on my face.
Vieni qui a sederti sulla faccia.

Suck my dick.
***Ciucciami** il cazzo.*
You can use *ciucciare*, *succhiare*, or *poppare* interchangeably.

Give me…
Dammi/Fammi…

a blow job.
un pompino.

fellatio.
il fellatio.

a B. J.
un bocchino.
Literally, "pacifier."

dome.
la cappella.
Literally, "chapel."

a blowey.
il sultano.

What a load!
Che sborrata!

Ejaculation
L'eiaculazione

Sperm
Lo sperma

Cum
La sborra

Cream
La panna

Jizz
Il brodo

To squirt
Schizzare

To blow your wad
Spegnere la candela
Literally, "to blow out the candle."

·····Balls
Le palle

The English anatomical term "testicles" comes from the
Latin *testiculi*, meaning "witnesses." Back in the day, a
man swore an oath on what he held most precious—his
family jewels—and that, *signore* and *signori*, is where we
get the word "testimony."

Balls
Palle; Coglioni

Ballsack
Broccoli
Literally like the vegetable.

Family jewels
Gioielli di famiglia

Berries
Caramelle
Literally, "candies."

Nuts
Castagne
Literally, "chestnuts."

Nads
Scatole

·····Pussy
La fica

No matter what you call it—pussy, box, snatch, vajayjay—you may find it interesting to know that the word "vagina" is Latin for "scabbard" or "sword sheath." Note that to sweeten up a term, Italians insert *bella*: *Che bella fica!* (What a nice pussy!) *Che bella gnocca!* (What a pretty little cunt!) *Che bella topa!* (What a nice little beaver!)

Lick my...
Lecca la mia...

Suck my...
Succhia la mia...

>**vagina.**
>*vagina.*

>**coochie.**
>*fischia.*
>Literally, "whistle."

>**cunt.**
>*fregna.*

>**bell.**
>*campana.*

>**box.**
>*scatola.*

>**Gina.**
>*Giovannina.*

>**hole.**
>*buco.*
>This was originally used in Napoletan and is very vulgar! Also refers to the other hole.

>**thing.**
>*cosa.*
>Also, *quella cosa* (that thing).

CREATURES)))
LE CREATURE

And in case you'd like to liken your ladyparts to your favorite animal:

bearded clam
lumaca
Literally, "snail."

bird
quaglia
Literally, "quail."

butterfly
farfalla ; farfallina

conch
conchiglia

cooter
passera ; passerina
Literally, "sparrow" and "little sparrow."

beaver
topa
Literally, "little mouse." This is used a lot in Tuscany and surroundings; *sorca* is also sometimes used.

nest
nido

nymph
ninfa

little mouth.
sticchio.
Sicilian, the feminine equivalent to the word *minchia*.

bucket.
secchio.

bush.
cespuglio.

guitar.
chitarra.

muff.
triangolino peloso.
Literally, "hairy triangle."

minge.
mussa.

snatch.
nassa.
Literally, "net."

slit.
fessa.
Very vulgar!

clit.
grilletto.

button.
bottone.

TO THE TABLE!)))
AL TAVOLO!

These are all table terms that have been used to describe pussy.
Buon appetito!

apricot
albicocca

goblet
bicchiere

cauldron
pentola

chestnut
castagna

crumpet
patatina
Literally, "little potato."

love box
trifola
Literally, "truffle."

bump
gnocca

prune
prugna

pumpkin
zucca

punani
paniere
Literally, "bread basket."

raisin
susina

salad
verdura
Literally, "vegetables."

tea cup
tazza

cup
coppa

oyster
cozza
Literally, "mussel."

Cunnilingus
Il cunnilingus

To eat pussy
Mangiare la micia

To reach orgasm
Raggiungere l'orgasmo

To stimulate the G-spot
Stimolare il punto G

To titillate with your tongue
Titillare con la lingua

·····The oldest profession in the world
Il mestiere più antico del mondo

La puttana (whore) has been selflessly providing services for as long as there have been lonely dicks in this world. The Romans even had special coins they used in exchange for sex.

The *cortigiane* (courtesans) were slightly different from *le puttane*; in addition to providing affection, they were enlisted as companions and conversationalists. Often women of lower status, they were as esteemed for their powers to seduce both *il corpo* (the body) and the mind. Today's escorts serve in much the same capacity, although it's doubtful they'll be quoting poetry to you.

Prostitution
La prostituzione

To procure services
Procurare servizi

A call girl
Una passeggiatrice

A courtesan
Una cortigiana

A harlot
Una meretrice

A ho
Una mignotta

A hooker
Una baldracca

A hussy
Una sgualdrina

A pimp
Un pappone

A prostitute
Una prostituta

Sex for hire
Sessinvendola

A slut
Una troia

A streetwalker
Una figlia del marciapiede
Literally, "a daughter of the sidewalk."

A tramp
Una bagascia

A whore
Una puttana

And the insults are not limited to girls gone wild. Here are a few monikers used to describe the male progeny of the whores, hussies, and sluts that gave birth to them.

A prodigal son
Un figliol prodigo

A son of a ho
Un figlio di mignotta

A son of a bitch
Un figlio di puttana

A son of a gun
Figlio di buona donna
Euphemism for figlio di puttana

zero
Un figlio di nessuno
Literally, "a child of no one."

·····Masturbation
Masturbazione

Don't worry, you won't grow cauliflower in your ears.
Going *assolo* (alone) is the most natural thing in the world.
Your Italian sex-ed teacher might have used the clinical
term *masturbazione*, but you'll also hear *autoerotismo*.
Whatever you call it, the Italians are no strangers to double
clicking the mouse or beating the one-eyed monster.

I like to...
Mi piace...

> **diddle.**
> *fare il ditalino.*

> **play the pipe.**
> *farsi una pipa.*

> **jerk off.**
> *farsi una sega.*
> Literally, "to do the saw."

> **to masturbate.**
> *masturbarsi.*

to spank the monkey.
scuotere l'arnese.
Literally, "jiggle the tool."

to take care of myself.
arrangiarmi da solo.

to touch myself.
toccarmi.

·····Love Italian style
L'amore italiano

Want to make someone *impazzire di piacere* (go crazy with pleasure)? Italy is a place where even a one night hookup can feel like *innamorarsi* (falling in love).

Let's…
Andiamo…

hug.
abbracciarci.

cuddle.
coccolarci.

snuggle.
rannicchiarci.

spoon.
fare il cucchiaio.

fondle each other.
palpeggiarci.

make love.
fare l'amore.

·····When things go bad
Quando le cose vanno male

All those high hopes, and then out of nowhere, things take a turn for the worse and you're left wondering, What went wrong?

We broke up.
Ci siamo separati.

She/he broke my heart.
Mi ha rotto il cuore.

My girlfriend dumped me.
La mia ragazza mi ha mollato.

My boyfriend left me.
Il mio ragazzo mi ha lasciata.

At least we had make-up sex.
Almeno abbiamo fatto la pace a letto.
Literally, "We made peace in bed."

We split a month ago.
Ci siamo lasciati un mese fa.

·····Yo' Casanova
Ciao Casanova

"What is life, without love?" asked the Venetian adventurer Giacomo Girolamo Casanova (1725–98) in his memoir *Histoire de ma vie* (Story of My Life)—the book described in copious detail his sexual conquests (122 recorded). Unable to keep his dick under control, he was often on the run in order to avoid going back to jail, a place he had spent considerable time. Not surprisingly, he is one of the first reported to use "assurance caps" (earlier forms of condoms) to both prevent syphilis as well as pregnancy.

He is...
Lui è...

> **a dick.**
> *una pirla.*
> Literally, "a pearl"

> **a flatterer.**
> *un lecchino.*
> Literally, "a little licker."

> **an impotent.**
> *un impotente.*

> **a limp dick.**
> *un rammolito.*

like a newbie.
come un eiaculazione precoce.
Literally, "a premature ejaculation."

a ruffian.
un ruffiano.

a show-off.
uno sborrone.

a sissy.
una femminuccia.

a voyeur.
un guardone.

a well-endowed man.
un ben dotato.

·····How's it goin', tiger?
Come va, tigre?

It's not what, but how something is said. *La mia zozzona* (mylittle tramp) can be quite a turn-on if you're both *nudi* (naked). It's another story if, on the other hand, she's the *sudiciona* (nasty bitch) that left you for your best friend.

You are such...
Sei proprio...

> **a tiger in bed.**
> *una tigre del materasso.*
> Literally, "a tiger of the mattress."
>
> **a great piece of pussy.**
> *una bella gnocca.*
>
> **a nice ride.**
> *una bella bicicletta.*
> Literally, "a beautiful bicycle."
>
> **a sex pot.**
> *una donnina allegra.*
> Literally, "a happy woman."

a sexual mentor.
una nave scuola.
Tends to be used to describe when an older, more experienced woman teaches the ropes to a younger man.

a slag.
una maiala.

a dirty bitch.
una sporcacciona.

a nasty bitch.
una sudiciona.

a cocksucker.
una bocchinara.

a tramp.
una zozza.

a prude.
una morigerata.

·····Contraception
Contraccettivi

The word "venereal" (as in, disease) derives from the love goddess Venus. Use an *impermeabile* (raincoat)! They come in all shapes, sizes, and *colori*. You can buy birth control at any *farmacia*, and you can often find condoms in vending machines outside clubs.

Do you have...?
Hai...?

a condom
un preservativo

a rubber
un profilattico

a balloon
un palloncino

pajamas
un pigiamino

a parachute
a paracadute

a Trojan
un goldone

You use birth control, right?
Usi l'anticoncezionale, vero?

Let's make a family—my biological clock is ticking.
Facciamo una famigila—il mio orologio biologico sta battendo.

You better put a raincoat on.
Devi metterti un impermeabile.

Use a glove.
Usa un guanto.

Got any lubricant?
Hai del lubrificante?

I brought protection.
Ho portato un profilattico.

I'm on the pill.
Prendo la pillola.

I use an IUD.
Uso la spirale.

I use a diaphragm.
Uso il diaframma.

Have you been tested for AIDS?
Hai mai fatto le analisi per l'AIDS?

Have you ever had a STI?
Hai mai avuto una malattia venerea?

Sorry to ask, but you don't have herpes, syphilis, or hepatitis C, do you?
Mi dispiace chiederti, ma non hai l'herpes, la sifilideou, o l'epatite C, vero?

·····Transgressions
Trasgressioni

Ancient Rome's history is a cornucopia of sex, *sadismo*, and madness. Dressed in leather harnesses with metal studs, gladiators were notorious for their rugged, bad-ass sex appeal in a libidinous public hungry for action. (Just imagine Russell Crowe and you might even long for the good old days).

Role-play and power games were a big turn-on for the sexually depraved Romans, and their graffiti, poetry, and *arte* were filled with pornographic depictions of raw, spiritless copulation, *dominazione*, and *sottomissione*. (Another reason Pompeii was such a popular destination before Vesuvius blew her wad and covered the ancient city in lava.)

The vulgar term *buggerone* is used to describe a top. The terms *buggioressa* and *buggeressa* refer to women who allowed themselves to be sodomized (more often than not as a means of birth control).

Bondage
La schiavitù

Bondage and discipline
Il bondage e la disciplina
Also abbreviated to B&D.

Swinger party
Lo scambio di coppia
Literally, "couple exchange."

Domination and submission
La dominazione e la sottomissione
Also abbreviated to D&S or DS.

Eroticism
L'erotismo

Fetishism
Il feticismo

SEX AND TOYS)))
IL SESSO E I GIOCATTOLI

Many Italian pharmacies now conveniently carry *vibratori* and other *oggetti sexy* (sexy objects), although they're not always on display. You'll have to go to the sexy shop for special accessories such as nipple clamps, *ferri* (handcuffs), and cock rings, if that's your thing.

a cock ring
un anello fallico ; anello per pene

a dildo
un dildo

a fake penis
un pene artificiale

handcuffs
le manette

a mask
una maschera

nipple clamps
le pinzette stringicapezzoli

a strap-on belt
una cintura per dildi

Ben Wa balls
le palline vaginali

Foot worship
L'adorazione del piede

Orgy
L'ammucchiata
Literally, "pile."

Sadism and masochism
Il sadismo e il masochismo
Also abbreviated to S&M or SM.

Sadomasochism
Il sado-maso

Safe, sound, and consensual
Sicuro, sano, e consensuale

Safeword
Parola di sicurezza

Submissive
Il/la sottomesso/a

Dominant
Il/la dominante

The top
Il/la top

Sodomy
La sodomia

Spank me!
Sculacciami!

I'm your slave boy.
Sono il tuo schiavo.

CHAPTER 6

ANGRY ITALIAN

ITALIANO ARRABBIATO

Italians are hyperbolic people: They can be the kindest, most *gentile* (nice) people on the planet, but they can also be vicious, hypocritical gossips. So if you want to be an Italian, along with learning to pander and oblige, you're going to have to learn how to swear like one. Gear up with a few insults and *minacce* (threats).

·····Pissed off
Incazzato

The eloquent expression *avere le palle piene* (to have full balls) sums up what happens when an Italian gets pissed off.

> **I'm really angry.**
> *Sono proprio **arrabbiato/a**.*

> **Be careful shithead!**
> *Sta' attento **testa di merda**!*

> **I'm fed up with this shit!**
> ***Mi sono stufato/a** con questa merda!*

🍷 THE GODFATHER

Revenge is a dish best served cold. So is this cocktail.

GET THESE:

  1½ ounces blended scotch

  ½ ounce amaretto

  lemon peel, for garnish

DO THIS:

Add both liquid ingredients to a rocks glass with ice. (Extra points if you cut your own ice with an ice pick.) Stir until well chilled and garnish with a lemon peel.

I'm fuckin' sick of this shit!
Ho le palle piene!
Literally, "my balls are full."

I'm really **ticked off**.
*Sono veramente **incavolato/a**.*

You're gettin' on my nerves.
Mi fai venire il nervoso.

You've got **a lot of nerve** shithead.
*Ha **una faccia tosta testa** di merda.*

Don't **piss me off**.
*Non **mi scazzare**.*

Okay, now **I'm pissed**!
*Adesso **sono incazzato/a**.*

What **are you ranting** about?
*Ma di cosa **stai delirando**?*

That poor bastard was so **raging mad** when he found his wife screwing his son's best friend.
*Si è **incazzato nero** quando ha trovato la moglie a scopare l'amichetto di suo figlio.*
The word *nero* literally means "black."

·····You talkin' to me?
Stai parlando a me?

When an Italian gets sick 'n' tired of being sick 'n' tired, all bets are off.

What's your fuckin' issue?
Mah, che cazzo hai?

You gotta problem with me?
Ce l'hai con me?

Don't bother me.
Non disturbarmi.

What the fuck do you mean by that?
Che cazzo intendi?

What the fuck do you want?
Che cazzo vuoi?

What'd you say? You wanna repeat that?
Che cosa hai detto? Lo vuoi ripetere?

Have you gone mad?
Sei divento/a matto/a?

Now you're goin' too far.
Adesso stai esagerando.

Do ya' think I was born yesterday?
Ma per chi mi hai preso?
Literally, "Who are you taking me for?"

Is it any of your damn business?
Che te ne frega?

Do you think I'm an idiot?
Mi stai prendendo per il culo?
Literally, "Do you take me for an ass?"

FUCK OFF!)))
VAFFANCULO!

If you have to choose one insult make it *Vaffanculo!* (pronounced *vaf-fahn-KOO-loh*). Note that in some dialects you will hear the "c" pronounced like a "g."

Literally meaning, "go do it in the ass," it can be employed when you spill *caffé* on your *camicia bianca* (white shirt), or discover your car has *una gomma a terra* (a flat). There's the *Vaffanculo!* you scream at your *stronzo* (turd) of a boss the day you get canned (probably for swearing too much). And there's the final *Vaffanculo!* you might utilize when you give your lying, cheating *amante* (lover) the kick in the ass he or she deserves. This particular version was even made into a national campaign *Vaffa-Day* (or "V-day") by the popular comedian and social activist Beppe Grillo to protest government corruption.

·····Go to hell
Va' al inferno!

Get out of here!
Vattene!

Go take a shit!
Va' a cagare!

Go to hell!
Va' all'inferno!

I hate you!
Ti odio!

Suck my dick!
Ciucciami il cazzo!

Go away!
Vai via!

Get outta here!
Vattene!

Get the fuck outta here!
Sparisci!

Motherfucker!
Porca puttana!

Shitface!
Faccia di merda!

Mind your own beeswax!
Fatti i fatti tuoi!
Literally, "Mind your own facts."

·····Smack talk
Sparlare

Unleash the catty bitch inside of you and smack around these nasty little *commenti*. We all know your *merda* don't stink, oh no.

I don't like to gossip but who does she think she is?
*Non mi piace **fare il pettegolo** ma chi pensa di essere?*

Is he gay?
È gay?

I hope not.
Spero di no.

I heard he has sex with men and with women.
Ho sentito che ha rapporti sessuali con uomini e con donne.

Do you wanna hear a rumor?
*Vuoi sentire **un pettegolezzo**?*

Quit talking nonsense.
*Non dire delle **sciocchezze**.*

She thinks she's all that.
Se la tira quella.

Did she get a boob job?
Si è rifatta/ritoccata il seno?
Literally, "redo" or "retouch."

No, worse. She was in the hospital because she had her sweet ass done…and it dropped!
No, peggio. Era in ospedale perché si è rifatta il suo culetto…e lo ha ceduto!

Ever since she did the Botox treatment, she can't get that smile off her face.
Da quando ha fatto il trattamento con botulino non riesce a togliersi il sorriso dalla faccia.

She's a moron. If you ask me, she was better off before.
È un carciofo. Secondo me stava meglio prima.
Italians use *carciofo* (artichoke) to describe someone who's not exactly the sharpest knife in the drawer.

Who knows if the bastard child is really his?
Chi sa se il bastardino è veramente suo?

It's enough to mention his name and she cries.
Basta pronunciare il suo nome e piange.

Don't be such a gossip.
Non essere un/a pettegolo/a.

·····Fightin' words
Parole di lotta

Let's face it, Italians are lovers, not fighters. Rarely do you see a group of drunk Italians getting into a brawl. Can *che abbaia non morde*. (The dog that barks doesn't bite.) They'll curse and stomp their feet until they're blue in the face, but in the end they're all talk. Now, Italian nonne (grandmothers) are another story. You're definitely asking for a smack across the face if you piss them off.

If you don't close your mouth, I'll split your head open.
Se non chiudi la bocca, ti spacco la testa.

I'm counting to three. If at two you don't shut the fuck up, at one I'm gonna hurt you.
Conto fino a tre. Se al due non ti zitti, all'uno ti gonfio.

There's a certain poetry to Italian threats. They don't just say, "Hey, I'm going to hit you." Instead, expect to hear things like:

Can you smell the stink from the bullshit that comes out of your mouth?
Ma la senti la puzza delle stronzate che dici?

Can your dick reach your asshole? If so, stick it up your ass!
Ti arriva l'uccello al buco del culo? Sì? Allora inculati!

If I had an ass like your face, I'd be ashamed to take a shit.
Se avessi il culo come la tua faccia, mi vergognerei ad andare a cacare.

If my dog had your face, I'd shave its ass and teach it to walk backward!
Se il mio cane avesse la tua faccia, gli raderei il culo e gli insegnerei a camminare al contrario!

WHAT A LOAD OF CRAP!)))
CHE CAZZATA!

All of these terms are used interchangeably by Italians to indicate their disbelief when hearing someone's bullshit story:

What...
Che...

crap!
cagata!

garbage!
cavolata!
Literally, "cabbage."

B.S.
puttanata!
From *puttana*, the word for "whore."

bull!
troiata!
From *troia*, the word for "slut."

bullshit!
stronzata!
From *stronzo*, the word for "turd."

If you're not careful, I'll stick my finger up your ass and turn you inside out like a sock.
Se non stai attento, ti infilo un dito in culo e ti rivolto come un calzino!

Shit into your hand and **slap yourself.**
*Cacati in mano e **pigliati a schiaffi.***

You truly have the face of an ass.
Hai proprio una faccia da culo.

Your **bad breath** is so gross that you kill flies midair.
*Il tuo **alito** è talmente schifoso che ammazzi le mosche al nvolo.*

You're so stupid your last neuron died of loneliness.
*Sei così **stupido** che il tuo ultimo neurone è morto di solitudine.*

You're such a **ball breaker** you'd need two of you to make one dickhead!
*Sei così **coglione** che ce ne vogliono due come te per fare una testa di cazzo!*

You're such **a turd** your mother shit you out.
*Sei così **stronzo** che tua madre ti ha cagato.*

·····Punches and kicks
Pugni e calci

I'm gonna hit you so bad you'll go back in time!
***Ti dò una sberla** che ti mando indietro nel tempo!*

I'll hurt you so bad that I'll get out of prison before you get out of the hospital.
***Ti farò talmente male** che uscirò prima io di galera che tu dall'ospedale.*

I'll kick your ass so hard your teeth will shatter.
***Ti tiro un calcio in culo** così forte che ti spacco i denti.*

Be careful or I'll…you.
Stai attento che ti dò…

> smack
> *una sberla*

> slap
> *uno schiaffo*

> hit
> *una botta*

If you try it with me, **I'll deck you!**
*Se ci provi, **ti tiro un ceffone!***

Does your mommy know you'll be spending the night in the hospital?
Lo sa tua mamma che stanotte dormi all'ospedale?

I'll break your legs.
Ti spezzo le gambe.

Do you really want to spend tomorrow **shitting the teeth** I made you swallow?
*Domani vuoi passare una giornata **cagando i denti** che ti ho fatto ingoiare?*

I'll rip your arms off and hit you with them!
Ti strappo le braccia e te le tiro addosso.

Don't make me bitchslap you!
Non farti dare uno schiaffone!

I'll grab you, break you, eat you, and shit you out right here!
Te prendo, te spezzo, te mangio, e te cago qua intorno!

WHAT A DRAG!)))
CHE PALLE!

Che palle! (Literally, "What balls!") is among some of the most commonly muttered slang in the Italian language. Italians who like to pretend they're above swearing may also use the term *Che pizza!* (What pizza!).

Che palle is used to express boredom, annoyance, and impatience in a variety of *situazioni* such as:

When the bottom of a soggy paper bag drops out and all the garbage with it...*Che palle!*

Your *professore* tells you you're having a pop quiz...*Che palle!*

Your *ragazza* (girlfriend) rags on you for not calling her...*Che palle!*

Your *ragazzo* (boyfriend) insists that it was "just sex" and meant nothing...*Che palle!*

•••••Insults
Sgarbi

Using only one insult would be like eating the same kind of pasta every day—it's better to have *varietà*.

Don't act like a dumbfuck.
*Non comportarti da **sciocco**.*

You know, you're a real fool.
*Sei proprio **scemo**, sai?*

He/She is a *retard*.
*Lui/Lei è un/a **cretino/a**.*

What a dumbass—he doesn't understand dick.
*Che **balordo**—lui non capisce un cazzo.*

That cheat punked me outta five bucks.
*Quell'**imbroglione** mi ha fregato cinque dollari.*

Ugh, what a bore.
*Uffa, che **noia**.*

He/She is...
Lui/Lei è...

You're acting like...
Ti comporti come...

> **a pain in the ass.**
> *un/a rompicoglioni.*
> Literally, "a ball-breaker."

> **a rude mother-fucker.**
> *un/a maleducato/a.*

> **a son-of-a-bitch.**
> *un figlio di puttana.*

> **a turd.**
> *uno/a stronzo/a.*
> This versatile word can simultaneously mean
> "dumbass," "schmuck," "jerk," and "ass-wipe,"
> depending on the user and how it's used.

> **a bastard.**
> *un bastardo.*

> **a bitch.**
> *una cagna.*

> **a brownnoser.**
> *un leccapiedi.*
> Literally, "a foot licker."

an oaf.
un cafone.

a slob.
uno sporcaccione.
Literally, "a big pig."

a dimwit.
un/a tonto/a.
This word likely originates from the character Tonto (as in The Lone Ranger).

a phony baloney.
un/a ballista.

a chump.
un/a burino/a.

a fake.
un'impostore.

a poser.
un pagliaccio.
Literally, "a clown."

a jokester.
un/a birichino/a.
A *birichinata* is a practical joke.

a liar.
un/a bugiardo/a.

a cocksucker.
un/a bocchinaro/a.

a pervert.
un/a porco/a.
Literally, "pig."

·····What a bitch
Che cagna

What a…
Che…

She is a major…
Lei è un/una proprio…

biotch.
troietta.
From the word *troia*.

bitch-ass.
disgraziata.

cock tease.
puttanella.
Derivative of the word *puttana*.

heifer.
vacca.

dog.
cammello.
Literally, "a camel," and used to refer to a very
unattractive woman.

ugly ass chick.
pugno nell'occhio.
Literally, "a punch in the eye."

hag.
marmitta.
Literally, "a marmot."

prude.
morigerata.

sneaky mother-fucker.
furbacchiona.
From the word *furbo/a* (sly); *la furbizia* refers to "slyness."

witch.
strega.

·····Loserville
Sfigati

This section is for your boss, your husband, your boyfriend,
your lover. He's the *bastardo* that cheated on you. He's the
briccone (asshole) at the DMV, the *stronzetto* (dipshit) who
busted you speeding, the *figlio di putana* (son-of-a-bitch)
who ate the last chocolate.

He's such a/an…
Lui è un vero…

I can't believe I ever slept with that…
Com'è possibile ho dormito con quel…

asshole!
briccone!

asswipe!
lecchino!

YOUR MOMMY AND SISTER…)))
TUA MAMMA E SORELLA…

This is where the real Italian comes out. Insulting someone's mother or sister is a shortcut to hell.

Your mother/sister is…
Tua mamma/sorella è …

so **ugly** she makes onions cry.
*così **brutta** che fa piangere le cipolle.*

so **stupid** that behind the door of the bar she always shits herself because of the word PUSH.
*così **stupida** che davanti alla porta del bar si caga sempre addosso perché c'è scritto SPINGERE.*

so **scary** that Parliament officially changed Halloween to her birthday.
*così **spaventosa** che il Parlamento ha ufficialmente spostato Halloween al giorno del suo compleanno.*

a fat pig.
una grassona.

gives blow jobs to dead dogs.
una che fa le pompe ai cani morti.

a whore.
una puttana.

a slut.
una troia.

So how's your mother and my children?
Come sta tua moglie e i miei figli?

WHAT THE DICK...?)))
CHE CAZZO...?

Fuck! *Cazzo!* The catch-all swear word for cock, dick, or prick is *cazzo*. This five letter word is used every-fuckin'-where, in the same way that "fuck" is used in English as an adjective, like "fucking bastard," or as a verb, like "Fuck you!," and as a noun, like "a fuck." Euphemisms for *cazzo* include *cavolo* (cabbage), *cacchio*, and *Kaiser*.

> You're a real...
> *Sei proprio un...*
>> dick.
>> *cazzo.*
>>
>> big dick.
>> *cazzone.*
>> This is also used to describe a poser.
>>
>> dickhead.
>> *testa di cazzo.*
>>
>> Fuck yeah!
>> *Cazzuto!*
>>
>> He could give a **goddamn** about her.
>> *Non gliene **importa un cazzo** di lei.*
>>
>> He doesn't do dick.
>> *Non fa un cazzo.*
>>
>> How **the fuck** should I know?
>> *Che **cazzo** ne so!*

cocklicker!
leccacazzi!

cocksucker!
pompinaio!

dickhead!
minchione!

dicksucker!
succhiatore!

dipshit!
stronzetto!

Holy fuck!
Cazzo di Budda!
Literally, "Buddha's dick."

It's not worth a rat's ass.
Non vale un **cazzo**.

I could give a flying fuck.
Non me ne **frega un cazzo**.

Mind your own fucking business.
Fatti i cazzi tuoi!

My ass!
Col cazzo che!
Used sarcastically to contradict something someone has said.

Quit busting my chops.
Non mi rompere il cazzo.
Literally, "breaking my dick."

That sucks.
Sono cazzi.
Literally, "They're dicks."

When hell freezes over.
Quando il cazzo fa l'unghia.
Literally, "When a dick turns into a finger."

You're bugging the shit out of me.
Mi stai sul cazzo.

idiot!
idiota!

pathetic losah!
sciagurato/a!

rascal!
mascalzone!

schmuck!
cornuto!

sucker!
gonzo!

tramp!
barbone!

You're a real Einstein!
Hai scoperto l'America!
Literally, "You discovered America!" This is a sarcastic
statement, Einstein!

·····He who sleeps with dogs, wakes up with fleas.
Che va a letto con i cani, si leva con le pulci.

You don't have to be a common *criminale* (criminal) to
be called one in Italy. While not officially swearing, the
following terms are all used to describe those deemed
unworthy (which includes just about everyone that isn't
famiglia.) Especially helpful the next time you get punked
by someone.

A criminal
Un criminale

A crook
Un ladrone

A delinquent
Un delinquente

A hustler
Un furbone

A lowlife
Un poco di buono

A gangsta
Un mafioso

An outlaw
Un fuorilegge

TALISMEN, AMULETS AND GOOD-LUCK CHARMS)))
TALISMANI, AMULETI, E PORTEFORTUNA

You've seen the little gold charms that some Italian men wear as amulets. *Le corna* (the horns) is both a superstitious and deflective gesture meant to throw off *il malocchio*, i.e., "the evil eye," as well as to poke fun at someone. Calling a man *cornuto* (cuckold) is like saying, "You suck so bad in bed that your woman had to get it somewhere else." (This will probably happen to you once your girlfriend discovers Italian men, and vice versa.) This Italian obscenity carries a lot of weight and is a major *offesa* (insult). To make the *corna* (horns), hold one hand up in front of you with the back of the hand facing out, and extend your index and pinkie fingers while clasping your middle and ring fingers with your thumb, heavy-metal style.

> The poor **schmuck** got played and didn't even know it.
> *Il povero **cornuto** aveva le corna ma non lo sapeva.*
> Literally, "The poor cuckold had horns but didn't know it."

> This plastic Nemo fish is my **good-luck charm.**
> *Questo pesce Nemo di plastica è il mio **portafortuna**.*

Back in the day, Roman boy children were given a *bulla* to ward off evil spirits. As an homage to the revered dick-gods, this small pouch was worn around the neck and contained various amulets made from bronze and gold, including miniature schlongs. Paying respect to the divine phallus was considered an important aspect of Roman culture. Making the *manus fica* or "fig sign," was a way of evoking of good luck. Today, the tradition continues as modern Italian men continue to don these good luck charms, usually in the form of the *peperoncino* (pepper).

A petty thief
Un ladruncolo
Literally, "The poor cuckold had horns but didn't know it."

A scumbag
Una carogna

A thief
Un ladro

A thug
Una teppista

A troublemaker
Un malvivente

A villain
Un villano

A wrongdoer
Un malfattore

·····My God!
Dio mio!

Consider *Dirty Italian* a manual on what not to say in church. As one might expect from a country with a church on every corner, Italian employs quite a few colorful blasphemies that could almost sound like prayers—*Oh Dio buono!*—except you're no priest and this is hardly a religious *esperienza*.

Although rarely enforced, it is actually a bonafide offense to *bestemmiare* (curse) in public. Aside from its moral implications, in Italy, taking the Lord's name in vain will get you more than a spaghetti lashing and could result in a misdemeanor charge.

By Jove.
Per Giove.

Bloody Christ!
Mannaggia Cristo!

Christ!
Cristo!

CURSED)))
MALEDETTO

The adjectives *maledetto/a* (cursed) and *dannato/a* (damned) can be used to exaggerate any situation, like "I'm crazy starving." (Or, if you live on the West Coast, "I'm hella starving.")

> I'm **hella** starving.
> *Ho una fame **maledetta**.*
>
> Quit with that **goddamn** music!
> *Smetti con quella **maledetta** musica!*
>
> I was **fucking** freezing.
> *Avevo un freddo maledetto.*
>
> I was **fucking** scared shitless.
> *Avevo una paura **maledetta**.*
>
> Where'd that **damned** dog go?
> *Dov'è finito quel **dannato** cane?*

Criminy!
Cribbio!
A euphemism for Cristo.

Beast God!
Dio bestia!

Dammit!
Mannaggia!

Devil!
Diavolo!

Dog God!
Dio cane!

For heaven's sake!
Per carità!

For the love of God.
Per l'amore di Dio.

Go to hell!
Va' all'inferno!

Go to the devil!
Va' al diavolo!

Goddammit!
Maledizione!

Jesus!
Gesù!

My God!
Dio mio!

Oh, Mother of God!
Madonna!

Mary's a pig!
Porca Madonna!
If you used this as a kid, it would get your mouth washed out with lye.

Pig god!
Porco dio!
Porco dio is VERY OFFENSIVE; euphemisms include *Porco due*! (pig two) and *Porco zio*! (pig uncle). Sometimes the "p" is eliminated to make the expression more palatable; the often controversial Prime Minister Berlusconi was known to utter *Orco Dio*.

Saint Mary!
Santa Maria!

Shit God!
Dio merda!

Gosh!
Zio!
A euphemism for *Dio*.

Virgin Mary!
Madonna vergine!

•••••Road rage
Aggressività al volante

Cut off? Tell him off! And if the driver can't hear you, you can always give him your middle finger (an international gesture that needs no translation). When he runs your car off the road and into a ditch, you can always use your thumb to *fare autostop* (hitchhike).

Use your turn signals, you piece of shit!
*Usa **le frecce**, pezzo di merda!*

Dumbass driving, peril thriving.
*Deficiente al **volante**, pericolo costante.*
The Italian rhymes, if you didn't already notice.

You're better off on a donkey.
Ti conviene tornare sull'asino.

You drive like a deaf old lady who forgot her
glasses and has the shakes.
*Guidi come una vecchietta senza occhiali, sorda e
tremolante.*

·····To swear or not to swear
Bestemmiare o non bestemmiare

These verbs and idiomatic expressions related to cussing
may come in handy one day when you're just sick 'n' tired
of listening to someone's filthy-shit-foul piehole. Just add
non in front of a verb to tell someone not to do something,
as in *Non bestemmiare, testa di cazzo!* (Quit it with the
dirty language, dickhead!)

a blaspheme
una bestemmia

a curse
una maledizione

a cuss word
una parolaccia

Quit cussin' you ugly, deficient piece of shit.
Non maledire brutto, deficiente pezzo di merda.

Quit swearin'!
Non bestemmiare!

Nut jobs swear at everyone.
I matti imprecano contro tutti.

**With that goddamn book *Dirty Italian*, you're
swearing like a sailor!**
Con quel maledetto libro Dirty Italian*, stai
bestemmiando come un turco!*
Literally, "to swear like a Turk."

·····Chill out
Rilassati

The Italians have a saying, *il vino si fa con l'uva*, which translates to "wine is made from grapes." Obviously, you've got to stomp on a lot of grapes to get the juice to make the wine. After all the arm waving and teeth clenching, isn't it time to make nice?

It's not worth it.
Non vale la pena.

Don't get yourself all worked up.
Non esagerare.
Literally, "Don't exaggerate."

Leave it alone.
Lascialo stare.

Let it go.
Lascia perdere.

Don't lose your head.
Non perdere la testa.

Calm down.
Calma.

Can't we agree to disagree?
Possiamo convenire di essere in disaccordo?

Can't we just get along?
Perchè non possiamo andare d'accordo?

Chill!
Tranquillo/a!
Literally, "tranquil."

For the love of mother, quit it!
Per l'amore di madre, basta!

I can explain everything.
Posso spiegare tutto.

I don't wanna argue.
Non voglio litigare.

It's not what it looks like!
Non è quello che sembra!

It's useless getting all worked up over such stupidity.
È inutile arrabbiarsi per una stupidaggine.

Let's make nice.
Facciamo la pace.
Literally, "Let's make peace."

Make love not war.
Fate l'amore, non la guerra.

Quit with the fighting; let's have a happy ending.
Basta con questi litigi; facciamo finire bene la storia.

We're on the same team.
Siamo sulla stessa squadra.

CHAPTER 7

POPPY ITALIAN

ITALIANO POP

Italians practically invented *il divertimento* (amusement) whether you're talking about *teatro* (theater), *musica* (music), film, or *la moda* (fashion). Beyond their love of art and fashion, when Italians are at home they're usually surfing the net and watching bad television right alongside the rest of us.

•••••Art
L'Arte

Don't be a dumb-ass *ignorante*. Take the time to bone up on by our *storia dell'arte* (art history). Italy hosts some of the most extraordinary artistic expressions the world has ever known; if you didn't even know that the word "Renaissance" means "rebirth," put the book down for a *minuto* and rethink your priorities.

Italians really do enjoy viewing their national treasures. (Besides, there's a lot more to exhibit at the *museo* than just art.) Study up on some Michaelangelo and Leonardo so you can spit some game at the museum-goer hotties. *Arte* anyone?

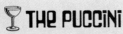# THE PUCCINI

Impress *la tua ragazza* with your amazing knowledge of opera—even if your knowledge only extends to this recipe. Hey, it's something.

GET THESE:

1½ ounces freshly squeezed mandarin orange juice

3½ ounces sparkling wine or champagne

DO THIS:

No cheating! Juice those mandarin oranges! Then pour the juice into a champagne flute. Top with champagne. Sip and feel the culture wash over you.

Wanna check out the museum?
*Vuoi andare al **museo**?*

Who's this artist? I like the way he painted those nudies.
*Chi è quest'artista? Mi piace come ha dipinto quei **nudi**.*

Isn't the Renaissance the name of a clothing store?
*Il **Rinasciamento** non è il nome di un negozio di abbigliamento?*

> **No, that's Rinascente, idiot.**
> *No, il negozio si chiama La Rinascente, idiota.*

Didn't they drink a lot during the Baroque?
*Non bevevano molto durante il **Barocco**?*

Look at the cute asses on those cherubs!
***Guarda** i culetti su quei putti!*

My dog could paint it better than that.
*Il mio cane **potrebbe** dipingerlo meglio.*

What a teeny weinie on that statue!
*Che pisellino su quella **statua**!*

You're joking, the Mona Lisa is called the Gioconda in Italian?
Scherzi, la Mona Lisa si chiama La Gioconda in italiano?

Why is that painting all fuzzy?
Perché quel quadro è tutto crespo?

> **That's called Impressionism, fool.**
> *Si chiama Impressionismo, scemo.*

I'm more into Gothic. It's all vampiry.
Mi va più il Gotico. È pieno di vampiri.

Abstract art is too…abstract for me.
L'Astrattismo è troppo…astratto per me.

How come there's pop art but no mom art?
Perché c'è la pop art ma non c'è la mamma Art?

Art is that which you can't understand it's significance, but you understand it has significance.
—Anonymous
Arte è ciò di cui non si capisce il significato, ma si capisce avere un significato. —Anonimo
A good one to use to impress the sophisticated ladies.

One should live their life as though it were a work of art.
Bisogna fare della propria vita come si fa un'opera d'arte. —Gabriele D'Annunzio
Gabriele knows his shit.

Artwork is always a confession.
L'opera d'arte è sempre una confessione. —Umberto Eco

·····Music
La Musica

When it comes to *musica*, rock still cracks open the skies and brings thousands of concert goers to the old cobble-stoned open *piazzas*. Lady Gaga and Sting regularly make the Italian circuit. Italian bands like Zucchero and Paolo

Conti still bring in aging rockers. Newer bands include Il *Pan del Diavolo* (The Devil's Bread), *Tre Allegri Ragazzi Morti* (Three Happy Dead Boys), and *Subsonica*. Other popular singers include Gianluca Capozzi, Pino Daniele, Giorgia, Jovanotti, Manuel Aspidi, Elisa, and Fabrizio Moro. Jazz, the blues, hip-hop, house, and reggae are all popular, too. And of course, Italians still weep for opera.

What kind of music do you listen to?
Che tipo di musica ti piace?

What's the name of that song?
Qual è il nome di quella canzone?

I can't listen to this crap!
Questa roba è inascoltabile!

I'd give anything to see some...
Darei un occhio per vedere...
Literally, "I'd give an eye."

Let's blast some...
Mettiamo un po' di...a palla.

I'm crazy about...
Impazzisco per...

> **pop**
> *la musica pop*
>
> **reggae**
> *la musica reggae*
>
> **hip-hop**
> *l'hip-hop*
>
> **house**
> *l'house*
>
> **jazz**
> *la musica jazz*
>
> **Latin-American**
> *la latino-americana*
>
> **techno**
> *la techno*

OPERA)))
L'OPERA

Move over Andrea Boccelli: Hotties like Patrizio Buanne draw scores of fans (and the occasional stalker). Italian opera has as much drama as a daytime soap. The lyricism and cadence of all those open vowels and trilled r's send shivers down the spines of even the tightest, most repressed of souls. Between the divas and *prima donnas* and the sopranos and the tenors, there's enough love, adultery, treachery, betrayal, and *ossessione* to keep Dante's inferno filled to the brim with sinners, horny noblemen, jilted lovers, and murderers. Add some instrumentals and your mood will be instantly enhanced, without the use of any mind-altering substances.

Opera singers got some pipes on them.
Le cantanti d'opera hanno un'ugola d'oro.

You're acting like a diva.
Ti stai comportando come una diva.

We got great seats in the balcony.
Abbiamo acquistato i posti sul balcone.

How much do I owe you for the tickets?
Quanto devo per i biglietti?

Is there an intermission? I'm gonna wet my pants.
C'è un intervallo? Sto per pisciarmi addosso.

God, I hate **pop punk**.
*Dio mio, odio il **pop punk**.*

Reggae music says we're all one. **It's a beautiful thing**, man.
La musica reggae *dice che siamo tutti uno.* ***Che bello,*** *amico.*

How come all house music **sounds the same**?
*Come mai tutta la musica house **è uguale**?*

Is it just Shakira, or are all Latin-American pop **singers** way hot?
*Ma è solo Shakira o tutte le **cantanti** latino-americane sono bone?*

Lady Gaga rocked that **concert** like nobody's business.
*Lady Gaga ha scatenato il **concerto** come nessun altro.*

The **show** sucked.
*Lo **spettacolo** faceva schifo.*

The *sound quality* was so shitty.
*La **qualità della musica** faceva proprio cagare.*

•••••Fashion
La moda

Style, flair, and poise are three words often used to describe those fashionable Italians. Ever since fig leaves were used to cover their privates, Italians have been fashion masters. *La moda* is as much a part of pop culture now as it was two thousand years ago when Roman women were temporarily put on budgets for how much money they could spend on their rags. Look for the words *vestiti* or *abbigliamento*—both refer to clothing.

SPEAK THE LINGO
Parliamo il linguaggio

Fashion is its own language, and the list of Italian words corresponding to fashion is extensive.

Skinny jeans are **in style** this year.
*I jeans attillati a sigaretta sonoTutto è **di moda** quest'anno.*

Big shoulders are definitely **out**.
*Le spalle larghe sono definitivamente **fuori moda.***
Or you can use the English word "out."

People **dress** very well in Italy.
*Si **vestono** molto bene in Italia.*

I **sported** my new kicks at the party last night.
*Per la festa ho **indossato** un'abito da sera.*

Here, try this on.
*Ecco, **prova questo**.*

Undress yourself in front of me right now!
***Spogliati** davanti a me subito!*

What size **do you wear?**
*Che taglia **porti**?*

What do you have on?
Che cosa ti metti?

Regardless of the money he spent, he's still a bad dresser.
Nonostante i soldi che ha speso, è ancora uno sfattone.

You look like a real redneck with those shoes.
Sembri proprio tamarro con quelle scarpe.

SEXY SEXY...
Sexy Sexy...

Sexy in Italy seems effortless, as though Italians were born knowing how to dress. Throw on an exquisite neck scarf, add a cashmere twin set, camel-colored cigarette pants, a string of pearls, and you're an Italian woman. Really cool eyewear doesn't hurt—designer glasses are *de rigueur*. Never get between an Italian and his Bulgari watch.

I fit into my old jeans!
*Sono rientrata nei **vecchi jeans**!*

Good God these pants are tight.
*Dio buono questi jeans sono **strettissimi**.*

Does this look good on me?
*Mi sta **bene** questo?*

Fine!
Togo!
Toghissimo makes it "Damn fine!"

It looks great on you!
*Ti sta **benissimo**!*

HOW TO UPDATE YOUR LOOK)))
COME AGGIORNARE IL VOSTRO LOOK

When in Rome, do as the Romans do and dress to impress! Even if your just going down to the corner store to get some orange juice, forget pajamas, your baggy sweatshirt, and your worn-out pair of Uggs. You're in Italy for fuck's sake. Show some respect! Here are a few fashion guidelines:

Tip#1: **Shoes**. Your *scarpe* tell more about you than anything else you're wearing. Ladies, forget about comfort. High heels were designed with two things in mind: to elongate the leg and accentuate the sway of hips. You don't walk in high heels—you strut!

Tip#2: **Jeans**. It's all about the ass. Try on a hundred pairs until you find the ones that cradle your buns like a welcome set of Italian man-hands. Buy three pairs and throw out everything that doesn't make you feel like a rock star the second you slip them on.

Tip#3: **Colors**. Italians aren't afraid of bright colors. Italian men regularly wear pink. You can add a touch of *fantasia* (a word that essentially means "imagination") to your wardrobe by simply adding the right accessory. Try on a slightly outrageous belt buckle or an oversized *borsa* (handbag). Let out your wild Italian child and put on a color you wouldn't normally wear.

Tip#4: **Accessories**. Find an *anello* (ring), *braccialetto* (bracelet), or an *orologio* (watch) that you can wear every day. Eventually it will feel like a part of you. You can never overaccessorize in Italy.

Tip#5: **Go easy on the fake stuff,** especially fake tans and artificial nails. There aren't a lot of nail salons in Italy, and Italians do not do French manicures. And no look is complete without a signature scent. Italy invented perfume, remember?

Out of this world!
È la fine del mondo!
Literally, "the end of the world."

You're a knockout!
*Sei uno **schianto**!*

Way hot!
Super bono/a!

You look gorgeous.
*Sei **bellissimo/a**.*

You're looking great!
Hai un aspetto magnifico!

Your ass belongs on a statue.
Hai un culo di marmo.
Literally, "You have a marble ass."

CLOTHES
I vestiti

I'm looking for...
Cerco...

I'd like to buy...
Vorrei comprare...

> **a belt.**
> *una cintura.*
>
> **a dress.**
> *un abito; un vestito.*
>
> **a jacket.**
> *una giacca.*
>
> **a sweater.**
> *una maglia.*
>
> **jeans.**
> *i jeans.*
>
> **a purse.**
> *una borsa.*
>
> **lingerie.**
> *della lingerie.*
>
> **pants.**
> *i pantaloni.*

FOR HER
Per lei

A couple of Italian bra tips: Bring the item you plan on wearing with you so that the sales lady can equip you with *il reggiseno giusto* (the correct bra). For maximum cleavage, you may opt for the Miracle bra, but you should also try on a *reggiseno invisibile* (invisible bra), made of silicone with clear plastic straps (or none at all); especially recommended for those of you endowed with the infamous bee-stings, in need of a little extra plungery.

A...bra
Un reggiseno....

> **push-up**
> *push-up*

> **sports**
> *sportivo*

> **balconette**
> *balconcino*

A thong
Un tanga

Underwear
Lo slip

Undies
Le mutandine

This bra is just right.
*Questo reggiseno è **giusto giusto**.*

Your tits look gigantic.
*Le tue tette sono **gigantesche**.*

Oh, it's not for me…I'm buying a present for my girlfriend.
*Oh, non è per me…compro un **regalo** per la mia ragazza.*

FOR HIM
Per lui

Briefs
I boxer briefs

Jock strap
Il sospensorio

Those boxers fit well.
Ti stanno bene i boxer.

CRAZY FOR BEAUTIFUL SHOES
Una mania per le belle scarpe

Now, whether you like it or not, we all have a place on the ladder of life, and to the Italians, *le scarpe* (shoes) say more about where our notch is than any other article. If you're a shoe-hound, designer boots are a must-have. Watch out! Because Italy is about to make your bank account its bitch.

I like to wear…
Preferisco portare…
Literally, "I prefer to wear…"

Do you have these...in my size?
Avete queste...nella mia misura?

I totally have a fetish for...
Ho la mania per...

> **tennis shoes**
> *le scarpe da tennis*
>
> **boots**
> *gli stivali*
>
> **heels**
> *i trampoli ; tacchi*
>
> **pumps**
> *le scarpe scollate*
>
> **high heels**
> *le scarpe con tacco alto*
>
> **lace-up shoes**
> *le scarpe allacciate*
>
> **pointed shoes**
> *le scarpe a punta*
>
> **sandals**
> *i sandali*
>
> **clogs**
> *gli zoccoli*
>
> **stilettos**
> *i tacchi a spillo*
>
> **stockings**
> *le calzatine*
>
> **tights**
> *i collants*
>
> **fishnet stockings**
> *le calze a rete*

I like to go barefoot.
*Mi piace andare **scalzo/a**.*

What beautiful ankles you have!
*Che belle **caviglie** hai!*

I have a foot fetish.
*Ho una **mania per i piedi**.*

I swear, she kept her **heels** on even in bed!
*Ti giuro, portava i **tacchi** anche a letto!*

Suck my **big toe**.
*Succhiami **l'alluce**.*

·····Television
La televisione

There's no better way to *ammazzare il tempo* (kill time) than by watching Italian *televisione*. On any given day, *fotomodelle* (models) with plumped lips and Botoxed foreheads share stories about their favorite *mutandine* (underwear). Newscasters that look like they just walked off the pages of *Vogue* discuss the *telegiornali* (news) of the day. Everyday folk sit in studio audiences and applaud on cue. Reality shows like *Il Grande Fratello* (Big Brother) and *Isola dei Famosi* (Island of the Famous) are big hits in Italy. After all, what better way to feel good about yourself than to watch a bunch of desperate, attention-grabbing strangers quibble, squabble, and bicker while well-positioned cameras record every bloody *minuto*. And there's nothing like watching Cesar Millan on his show *The Dog Whisperer* (dubbed in Italian of course).

What do you wanna **watch**?
*Cosa vuoi **guardare**?*

What **TV shows** do you like?
*Che **programmi** ti piacciono?*

I was **channel surfing** when I came across some real artsy porn.
*Facevo **zapping** quando ho visto un film porno proprio artistico.*

What **channel** is that on?
*Su quale **canale** gira quel programma?*

FYI, the remote stays in my possession.
*Per la tua informazione, il **telecomando** rimane in mio possesso.*

Do you wanna fuck or watch TV?
*Vuoi scopare o guardare **la TV**?*
Note that TV is pronounced tee-voo.

Let's fuck first, and then watch television, okay?
Scopiamo e poi guardiamo la televisione, vabbene?

·····The movies
Il cinema

The Italians became obsessed with cinema almost as soon as the first projectors started making their way down to Italy from France back at the turn of the century. In those days, there were no vats of popcorn or gallons of soda; people watched from their terraces and the town's *piazza* as *lo spettacolo* was projected onto the sides of the medieval and ancient buildings (watch the Italian movie *Cinema Paradiso* to get an idea). In 1914, the first major silent picture, *Cabiria*, came out by Giovanni Pastrone, and it was notably one of the most important milestones in cinematic history. The impact those early flicks had on the Italian psyche has never left them.

Let's see a movie.
Andiamo a vedere un film.

What are the show times?
*Quale sono gli **orari dei film**?*

How long is it?
Quanto dura?

I prefer to watch movies on the big screen.
*Preferisco guardare i film sul **grande schermo**.*

What kind of movies do you like?
Che film ti piacciono?

COOKiNG SHOWS)))
PROGRAMMI DI CUCINA

The best part of Italian television are the *programmi di cucina* (cooking shows) like *La Prova di Abilità* ("The Ability Challenge") where winners get a chance to dine with their favorite *cantanti* (singers) or *Stelle e Padelle* ("Stars and Pans," a play on the fact that in Italian these two words rhyme) where *sfidanti di gara* (game contestants) fight for the chance to open their own *ristorante* or have their *ricette* published in a book. *Il Mondo di un Bicchiere* ("The World of the Glass") discusses everything involving drinks, mostly *il vino*, of course. *Pizza Passione* is a no-brainer. *Con i Piedi per Terra* ("With Feet on the Ground") talks about Italian agriculture, the Slow Food Movement, and visiting Italy's many regions, all each with their own special *cucina*. And finally, imported directly from the States, *Top Chef* is watched by millions of Italians every week, many of whom are probably not eating anything nearly as good as what they're seeing prepared.

I'm into…
Mi va…

comedy.
commedia.

drama.
drammatico.

horror.
horror.

animation.
animazione.

adventure.
avventura.

independent.
indipendente.

action.
azione.

biography.
biografico.

documentary.
documentario.

erotic.
erotico.

musical.
musicale.

pulp.
giallo.
"Yellow" films got their name from the fact that
schmaltzy paperback crime novels and mysteries were
typically identified by a yellow cover.

science fiction
fantascienza

skin flicks
film blu
Literally, "blue films." Books considered risqué were
identified by their blue covers when the printing of
paperbacks made books much more accessible to the
general population.

•••••Communications
Le comunicazioni

These days, staying in touch (and getting some action) has
never been easier. Millions of Italians surf the web, chat,
blog, and text 24/7. Making a date is as simple as flipping
open your *telefonino*. In addition to meeting new people
through existing friends, the Italians regularly use the
annunci (personals).

AT THE INTERNET CAFÉ
Al Internet café

Italians like to chat, and they use the English word with
an Italian twist—*chattare*. But beware: This has become
synonymous with sexting, and it won't be long before
you're being asked come *e dove ti piace* (how and where
you like it).

Is there an Internet café nearby?
C'è un café Internet qui vicino?

Where can I...
Dove posso...

> **check** my e-mail?
> ***controllare*** *la mia posta elettronica?*
> Italians also use the English word "e-mail."

> **download** a file?
> ***scaricare*** *un file?*
> Italians also like to use their version of the English, *daunlodare.*

> **browse** the web?
> ***navigare*** *nella rete?*
> Italians also use the term *surfare*, as in the old-school "surf the net."

What's your e-mail address?
*Qual è il tuo **indirizzo e-mail**?*

What site was that?
*Che **sito** era quello?*

Send me a picture.
*Invia una **foto** a me.*

Send me the link please.
*Mandami il **link** per favore.*

ℓ-MAIL)))
E-MAIL

In Italian, the "at" (@) symbol used in e-mail addresses is called *chiocciola* (pronounced *KYOH-choh-lah*), which means "snail." The "dot" is simply *punto*, which means "period."

> **My e-mail address is dirtyitalianbook at yahoo dot com (dirtyitalianbook@yahoo.com).**
> *Il mio indirizzo e-mail è dirtyitalianbook chiocciola yahoo punto com.*

Don't forget to back up the files.
*Non dimenticare di **backuppare** i file.*

Do you like to chat on the Internet?
Ti piace ciattare in rete?

It costs less to Skype than to use a phone.
Costa di meno Skypare che telefonare.
As you've probably noticed, Italians use a lot of English slang, enough that you might wonder, with all these English terms why bother with the Italian (you ethnocentric bonehead)?

THE TELEPHONE
Il telefono

Sit anywhere long enough and you'll hear someone's *telefonino* (aka *cellulare*) beep, sing, and vibrate. It could be yours. Italians answer the *telefono* in Italy with *Pronto!* (Ready!)

What's your number?
Qual è il tuo numero di telefono?

I'll give you a ring.
Ti faccio uno squillo.

Can I call you?
Ti posso telefonare?

Hello!
Pronto!

Hi, it's me.
Ciao, sono io.

Fantastic! Is Peter there?
Fantastico! C'è Pietro?

▪▪▪▪▪Seriously SMS
Sul serio SMS

Italians are maniacal texters and utilize their own special codes and shortcuts. *Mandare un SMS* (to send a text) is as common as speaking. Multitaskers like to text while driving through city *traffico*. (Given it's preponderance, it's a fuckin' *miracolo* they don't crash into each other more often.) Each text costs between seven and fifteen *centesimi*, and it can quickly add up. Because every character counts, certain commonly used words are abbreviated.

The letter "k" usually replaces ch, such as in *che* (what), like a *ke ora* (at what time).

The word *sei* (you are) is substituted with the number *sei* (6), like 6 *a casa*? (Are you home?)

The number 1 is used in lieu of the indefinite article *un* (a/an).

The letter "x" replaces per (including the preposition meaning "for"). *Perché* becomes xché or *xké* (why).

Vowels are dropped whenever possible: c (*ci*), cm (*come*), cmq (*comunque*), cn (*con*), dv (*dove*), m (*mi*), nn (*non*), qnd (*quando*), sn (*sono*), t (*ti*).

ITALIAN ABBREVIATIONS
Abbreviazioni italiane

Texting is a language unto itself. If you're chatting online or someone sends you a text, you can consult this handy little glossary to understand what they've just said.

BiMBOiTUS)))
BIMBOMINKIA

Bimbominkia is an exclusively tongue-in-cheek Italian term that comes from two words: *bimbo* (baby, or doll) and *minchia* (dick). The phenomenon usually afflicts angry bored teens whose lives consist of nonstop texting, posing, and other idiocies usually associated with this age bracket.

fdv	*Felice di vederti.*	Nice to see you.
risp	*Rispondimi.*	Answer me.
d6	*Dove sei?*	Where are you?
x fv	*Per favore.*	Please.
midi	*Mi dispiace.*	I'm sorry.
rds	*Ride da solo.*	LOL.
fct	*Fatti i cazzi tuoi.*	Mind your own fuckin' business.
ttp	*Torno fra poco.*	BRB.
ap	*A presto.*	C U soon.
sdr	*Sogni d'oro.*	Sweet dreams.
to	*Ti odio.*	I hate you.
hobidite	*Ho bisogno di te.*	I need you.
ta	*Ti amo.*	I love you.
mmt+	*Mi manchi tantissimo.*	I miss you so much.
tipe	*Ti penso.*	I'm thinking of you.
ba	*Bacio.*	Kiss.
xxx	*Tanti baci.*	A bunch of kisses.
ba&ab	*Baci e abbracci.*	Kiss and hugs.
abecba	*Abbracciami, eccitami, baciami.*	Hug me, excite me, kiss me.
™	*Tesoro mio.*	My treasure.
am	*Amore.*	Love.
aminfi	*Amore infinito.*	Infinite love.
tulanoins	*Tutta la notte insieme.*	All night together.
6 la +	*Sei la migliore.*	You're the best.

| 610 | *Sei uno zero.* | You're a loser. |
| amxse | *Amore per sempre.* | Love forever. |

·····Gestures
I gesti

Due to the fact that many people still speak local dialects, some of which are largely incomprehensible to people from other parts of the country, Italians are notorious for their expressive body language and gestures. These ought to get you started.

Basta! (Enough!)
Rub your hands together as if you were washing them.

Bellissimo! (Wonderful!)
Kiss you fingertips.

Che furbo. Attenzione! (What a sneak. Pay attention!)
Point your index finger to below your eye, and gently pull the bottom lid.

Che palle. ("What balls," used to indicate boredom.)
Make an inverted L with the thumb and index fingers of both hands. With your index fingers pointing down, shake your hands up and down.

Che sfiga! (What shit luck!)
Grab your family jewels and raise your eyebrows.

Delizioso! (Delicious!)
Place your index finger on the corner of your mouth and turn it back and forth.

Ho fame. (I'm hungry.)
Take your open-palmed hand and jab it into the side of your hip.

Madonna mia. (Oh brother!)
Bring your hands together as if you were praying, and tilt them up and down.

Me ne frego. (I could give a damn.)

Flick your fingers outward from your chin while slightly tilting your chin.

Mi dispiace. (No can do. I'm sorry.)

Make an L with your thumb and index finger (of both hands). Keeping the L formed, turn your thumbs outward and back several times.

Ti faccio un culo così! (I'll kick your ass!)

Take both hands and form a circle with your index fingers and thumbs. Shake up and down.

Vaffanculo! (Up yours!)

Place one hand inside the elbow of the opposite arm. Snap the opposite arm up with your hand open. I'm sure you're already familiar with this one...

Cornuto ("Shmuck," used to call someone a cuckold.)

Here you are imitating horns. Touch your middle and ring fingers to your thumb leaving your index and pinky fingers out like a tiny pair of horns. Lock your thumb around your tucked middle fingers. To express "knock on wood," make the same sign and point downward.

CHAPTER 8

SPORTY ITALIAN

GLI SPORT ITALIANI

On Sundays of course, there's the church, and then there's soccer. If the local team wins and you're in a major city, don't be surprised to find yourself stuck in *traffico* while Italians blow their horns, wave their arms, and scream like hell. Modern Italians are an active bunch, and besides soccer, they're at the *palestra* (gym) working out, playing tennis, or throwing around some cards. And of course, ever since the chariot games, spectators around the world can thank the Italians for combining speed with class—think Maserati, Ferrari, Ducati—not to forget the world-class bicycle race Giro d'Italia.

·····Sports

Gli sport

Italians stay current by reading *La Gazzetta dello Sport*, a newspaper completely *dedicato* to sports.

What sports do you like?
Che sport preferisci?

Why don't we go play…?
Perché non andiamo a giocare…?

♈ CAFFÈ CORRETTO

You are going to watch the World Cup regardless of the time zone. So if you have to get up at 3 a.m. to cheer for the Italian team, so be it. Just make your coffee a *caffè corretto* and you'll get a little extra jolt of excitement.

GET THESE:

> 1 shot fresh espresso
>
> sugar, optional
>
> 1 ounce grappa

DO THIS:

Make yourself a shot of espresso. Add sugar, if so desired. Then add the grappa. Sip and sing your heart out for the team.

I do...
Faccio...

I play...
Io gioco...

Let's watch some...
Guardiamo un po' di...

> **baseball.**
> *il baseball.*
>
> **basketball.**
> *la pallacanestro.*
> Or the Americanized *il basket* is also used.
>
> **boxing.**
> *la boxe.*
>
> **chess.**
> *gli scacchi.*
>
> **cycling.**
> *il ciclismo.*
>
> **dancing.**
> *la danza.*

football.
il futball americano.

golf.
il golf.

hockey.
l'hockey.

inline skating.
il pattinaggio inline.

jogging.
il footing.

Pilates.
Pilates.

Ping-Pong.
il ping pong.

racing.
la corsa.

soccer.
il calcio.
Literally, "the kick"; *il futball* is also used.

skateboarding.
il monopattino.

swimming.
il nuoto.

tennis.
il tennis.

weightlifting.
il sollevamento pesi.

weight training.
i pesi.
Short for *la pesistica.*

wrestling.
la lotta libera; wrestling.

yoga.
lo yoga.

·····Soccer
Il calcio

Veni, Vidi, Vici (I came, I saw, I conquered).You may not think Latin has a lot going for it, since it's been a dead language for several centuries, but if you don't want to sound like a complete moronic ass, do familiarize yourself with the above Latin expression, especially if you're a sports hound. Whether you're talking about sex or sports, this notorious Roman quotation still applies to Italy's national pastime. It's no understatement to say that Italians take their games *molto* seriously.

It's not hard to imagine that yesterday's *gladiatori* (gladiators) are today's *calciatori* (soccer players). The French, Spanish, and Brazilians may wince, but it's true—the Italian team is the dirty best (and most beautiful) in the *mondo*. If you think the Super Bowl is a big deal, wait until you see *milioni* of Italians leaving work early in order to watch the World Cup. When Italy plays, it's essentially a national *festa* (holiday).

Let's go to the game.
*Andiamo alla **partita**.*

What's your favorite team?
*Qual è la tua squadra **preferita**?*

The crowd was nuts.
*La **folla** era pazzesca.*

For the fans, soccer is practically a religion.
*Per i **tifosi**, il calcio è praticamente una religione.*

I'd like to buy a game card.
*Vorrei comprare una **schedina**.*

It should be quite a match this weekend.
*Dovrà essere un **campionato** strafigo questo weekend.*

Soccer players are like gods in Italy.
__I calciatori__ in Italia sono come gli dei.

A challenge
Una sfida

A free kick
Un calcio di punizione

A head butt
Una testata

A pass
Un lancio

A penalty kick
Un calcio di rigore

A player
Il giocatore

A shot
Il tiro

A tie game
Un pareggio

Winning/losing games
Vinte/perse

The ball
Il pallone ; La palla ; La sfera
La sfera literally means "the sphere."

The coach
L'allenatore

The defender
Il difensore

The forward
L'attaccante

The goalie
Il portiere

The mass
La massa

The mob
La turba

The ref
L'arbitro

The soccer field
Il campo di calcio

The stadium
Lo stadio

The sweeper
Il libero

·····Way to go!
Forza!

If you really want to be Italian, join the *tifosi* (fans) and sing for your favorite team, or curse the competition. You should know that the two main *serie* (series) are A and B. This is where the top Italian teams compete. A lot of the players from *Serie A* end up on the national team. Playing the numbers is big business, and everyone has a favorite team. For example, the *Laziali* are fans of the Lazio football club, while the *Rossoblu* (red and blue) are loyal to Bologna. In Milan, you'll hear the rants and raves of the *Rossoneri* (red and black), while the *Bianconeri* (white and black) are devotees of Juventus—you get the picture. Try screaming some of the following cheers and jeers to egg on your *squadra* (team).

Come on!
Dai!

Go for it!
Evvai!

Nice goal!
Bel goal!

Excellent!
Bravo!

Here we go.
Ora ci siamo.

You're making me wet myself!
Che orgasmo!
Literally, "What orgasm!"

Well done!
Bravo!

Hot damn, what a game!
Ammazza che partita!

·····Crazy for "kicks"
Matto per il calcio

As brilliant as the Italians are when making verbal love, they are equally gifted when it comes to spitting out insults and sputtering curses. Slam, sneer, and snub the opposition using these multipurpose invectives. Smear some paint on your face, throw your arm up with your hand clenched in a fist and yell as loud as you want, *BASTARDO FIGLIO DI PUTTANA TESTA DI MERDA VAFFANCULO* (bastard, son-of-a-bitch, shithead, fuck off!)…and let it all out, *bambino mio*. For every goddamn little thing that you've been keepin' tucked deep inside you, now is the time to release. Here, you get to use your outside voice. Holla!

Your team **sucks**!
*La vostra squadra **fa schifo**!*

The ref is a turd.
***L'arbitro** è uno stronzo.*

Hey ref, you're a schmuck!
Arbitro cornuto!

He fucked up.
Ha fatto una cazzata.

Here comes **trouble**.
*Arrivano i **guai**.*

We've had it with this game.
Ci siamo rotti con questa partita.

What a **shitty game**.
*Che **partita di merda**.*

This game sucked.
Questa partita è stata uno schifo.

He was kicked off the team for swearing.
***È stato espulso** dalla squadra per bestemmie.*

The Italian team **whooped** the French team.
*La squadra Italiana **ha fatto polpetta** della squadra Francese.*
Literally, "made meatballs out of."

Kick the ball!
***Tira** la palla!*

GiDD YUP Li L' HORSi@: THE PALiO)))

ANDIAMO A CAVALL O: IL PALIO

Since the thirteenth century (when men were still totally cool with wearing tights), the Palio in Siena has enjoyed a reputation for being one of the most corrupt *corsa da cavalli* (horse races) in the world. Winning is everything, and it doesn't matter what methods you use. It's like capitalism for sports: Playing dirty, fixing races, and cutting bribes are all par for the course.

The race takes place in Siena's central Piazza del Campo, where loads of dirt are trucked in to form the track. Every July and August, over 50,000 *spettatori* (spectators) come to watch the races, which begin with huge *processioni* (processions) of trumpet players, drummers, and flag bearers representing the colors of their *contrada* (district).

Only ten *contrade* are chosen by lottery to participate in a given race. The horses are also drawn by lottery and assigned to the participating districts, preventing (theoretically) any attempts to disable a prized steed. *I fantini* (jockeys) aren't even essential to win. If a horse arrives at the finish line without its jockey, its *contrada* still wins.

If you get a chance to visit Siena during the races, don't let anything keep you from screaming for your favorite contrada and calling the competition's sisters a bunch of *puttane* (whores).

> **Go back** to your mommy!
> *Torna dalla mamma!*
>
> Your **jockey** is a little turd!
> *Il vostro **fantino** è uno stronzetto!*

Come on...score a goal already!
Ma dai...segna un goal!

The French took a **beating** from the Italians—as usual.
*I Francesi sono stati **massacrati** dagli Italiani—come sempre.*

·····Workin' out
Fare la ginnastica

There are plenty of places to get your blood pumping in Italy— you've got your *palestra* (gym), your cycling courses, and your rock-climbing walls. Lots of Italians are hippied out now, and regularly do yoga, karate, Pilates, spinning, and *meditazione* (meditation).

Let's go to the gym.
Andiamo in palestra.

Want to go lift?
Vuoi andare a farti quattro pesi?

Can you spot me?
Puoi controllarmi?

Exercise helps reduce my cellulite.
La ginnastica aiuta a diminuire la cellulite.

He's/She's totally...
È completamente...

> **cut.**
> *definito/a.*
>
> **huge.**
> *enorme.*
>
> **ripped.**
> *muscoloso/a.*
>
> **sculpted.**
> *scolpito/a.*
>
> **toned.**
> *tonico/a.*

I want to work out my...
Voglio concentrarmi su...

> **abs.**
> *gli addominali.*
>
> **arms.**
> *le braccia.*

ass.
il culo.

back.
la schiena.

biceps.
i bicipidi.

glutes.
i glutei.

legs.
le gambe.

pecs.
i pettorali.

triceps.
i tricipidi.

Check out my **six-pack**. It's a situation.
*Guarda la **tartaruga**. È una situazione.*
Literally, "turtle."

Do you know where I can find a good **dance studio**?
*Sai dove posso trovare uno **studio di danza**?*

For every diet you gotta **burn the fat**.
*Per un programma dimagrante è necessario **bruciare i grassi**.*

How do Italians manage to eat so well and still have **lean legs** and a **flat stomach**?
*Come fanno gli Italiani a mangiare bene ed anche ad avere le **gambe snelle** e gli **addominali piatti**?*

How do you **stay in shape** without going to the gym?
*Come **rimani in forma** senza andare in palestra?*

It depends on your **metabolism**.
*Tutto dipende dal proprio **metabolismo**.*

It's all about **posture, breathing**, and **exercise**.
*È tutta una questione di **postura, respiro,** ed **esercizio**.*

·····Games
I giochi

The Italian expression *il dolce far niente* essentially translates to "the sweetness of doing nothing." In other words, hanging out. This takes practice, especially if you're a workaholic North American accustomed to two weeks' vacation and fifty-hour work weeks. *Il dolce far niente* implies a certain connoisseurship for relaxation. Especially now that the world economy has turned to shit, if there's ever a place to enjoy the here and now, it's Italy. There will always be difficult times, but somehow, with a good bottle of wine and the right company, it's not so bad.

Backgammon
La tavola reale

Pool
I biliardi

Cards
Le carte
Scopa is a very popular game with cards that resemble the tarot. This word is not to be confused with *una scopata*, which means "a fuck."

Checkers
La dama

Chess
Gli scacchi

Poker
Il poker

·····Video games
I giochi video

Italians aren't exactly known for being gamers like you see in the United States and Japan. Most young Italians hit the *sala di giochi* (arcade), although these days, most Italians are getting their fix with *giochi online* (online games).

Do you have a...?
Avete...?

PlayStation
Playstation

Xbox
X-Box

Nintendo
Nintendo

Wii
Wii

Yo, pass the controller.
*Dai, passami il **comando**.*

Use the trigger to kill those little green things.
*Schiaccia il **grilletto** per ammazzare quelle cosine verdi.*

Why would Princess ever date Mario? He's a short, little, fat dude with a '70s porn mustache.
Ma perchè mai la Principessa uscirebbe con Mario? È un tappo chiatto con i baffi stile pornostar degli anni Settanta.

Yeah, but he's a total hipster!
Sì, ma lui è proprio un uomo hipster!

CHAPTER 9

HUNGRY ITALIAN
ITALIANO AFFAMATO

Everyone loves to eat, but Italians live to eat. They spend more time on meals—shopping, preparing, and cleaning up after them—than anything else. Is it any surprise that Italians even have *gelato per i cani* (ice cream for dogs)?

For the *prima colazione* (breakfast), most Italians eat a *brioche* (pronounced *bree-OSH*) and wash it down with a *cappuccino* or *latte macchiato*. Thanks to Starfucks, you should be familiar with these common Italian beverages.

Il pranzo (lunch) is another story. You'll be hard-pressed to find a soul who works through the midday break, which usually consists of *un piatto* (a plate) of pasta or a bowl of soup and *un bicchiere di vino* (a glass of wine). *La cena* (dinner) is eaten later in Italy. Most *ristoranti* (restaurants) aren't even open before 7:00 p.m., and that's still considered on the early side.

🍸 LIMONCELLO

You had the *antipasto*, you had the *primi*, the *secondi,* and the *dolce*. Now you have a giant full belly and the *cameriere* may have to roll you out of the restaurant. Never fear. Order the classic digestif limoncello to help aid in digestion.

GET THIS:
    1½ ounces limoncello

DO THIS:
Keep your bottle of limoncello in the refrigerator so it's always nice and cold when you want to have some. Pour into a small sherry glass and sip after a meal. You'll feel so much better.

•••••Hunger
La fame

Italians use the word *affamato* to say "hungry"; *la fame* describes "hunger," whether it's the kind involving your dirty stomach or the type that has to do with your second *chakra* (that's the groin region, FYI).

Are you hungry?
Hai fame?

I'm sooooo hungry.
Ho tantissima fame.

I could eat a horse.
Sono proprio allupato/a.
Allupato can mean "hungry" as well as "horny" and comes from the word *lupo* (wolf), an animal given a lot of clout in Italy. For example, you'll also find the wolf in the phrase *Ho una fame da lupo* ("I'm hungry as a wolf"). Every guidebook will remind you of the fact that Romulus (who founded Rome) and his twin, Remus, were suckled by a she-wolf.

I could die from hunger!
Potrei morire dalla fame!

I'm dying of thirst!
Sto morendo di sete!

I'm friggin' starving!
Ho una fame da morti!
Literally, "I have a hunger of the dead."

Have you already eaten?
Hai già mangiato?

It's chow time!
A tavola!
Literally, "to the table."

Let's eat!
Mangiamo!

What are you in the mood for?
Cosa ti va?

I'm in the mood for...
Mi va...

Thanks, but I'm on a diet.
*Grazie, ma sono a **dieta**.*

Why don't we have a drink?
*Perché non ci facciamo una **bevutina**?*

·····Delicious
Delizioso

Everybody in Italy knows how to sing the "Ave Maria," but it's equally important to sing praises to the chef.

Compliments to the chef!
***Complimenti** al cuoco!*

Delicious!
Delizioso!

Incredible!
Incredibile!

It's amazingly good.
È buonissimo!

Taste it!
Assaggialo!

You've gotta try this!
Dai, prova questo!

Outta this world!
Fuori mondo!

This dish is like an *orgasm in my mouth*.
*Questo piatto è come un **orgasmo nella bocca**.*

This pizza is really good.
*Questa pizza è **buonissima**.*

Scrumptious!
Squisito!

Yummy!
Che buono!

I ate like a whale.
*Ho mangiato come una **balena**.*

GOING DUTCH)))
ALL A ROMANA

The concept of dividing the check, figuring out each person's intake, and calculating the *mancia* (tip) doesn't jive in Italy. Say you're broke and trying to conserve your Euro, so you order a lousy *insalata* (salad). In the meantime, your traveling companion orders the full *Monte*: *antipasto*, a plate of pasta Bolognese, a side of the much coveted and very expensive *tartufi* (truffles—not the chocolate kind, you moron, the mushroom kind that sells for 2,250 Euro for 1 kilo or about 2 pounds), and a choice cut of *vitello* (veal). He tops it with a *bottiglia* of Brunello di Montalcino, arguably one of Italy's finest wines.

You didn't order wine, but there's a *bicchiere* (glass) in front of you, and someone fills it. You all clink while chanting *Cin cin!* Your Italian tablemates ask you if you're hungry. You tell them no, lying through your teeth, because the truth is, you could devour the *tavolo*. You try to make your *insalata* last as long as you can while filling up on the *pane*. The table is cleared. *Un dolce?* asks the *cameriere*. He brings over a cart that is piled with pastries and little dainty tarts. Don't forget the coffee.

The *conto* (check) comes. Italians are by far some of the most generous people on the planet. Chances are someone in a position to do so will insist on picking up the tab and in response to your protests, they'll reassure you that it'll be your turn when they come to visit; for now, you're a guest in their country.

But what happens when you're with your classmates and everyone's fucking broke? If you throw in what you think you owe, someone else is gonna have to make up for it. The heathen that ordered the damned *tartufi* and *vino* is half drunk, giving hugs like he's Padre Pio. And so, to avoid looking like a total cheap-ass loser schmuck, you do as the Italians do, and split the bill evenly. Now, instead of your paying 10 Euro, you're borrowing cash from your *compagno di stanza* (roommate) to throw in 70 Euro, the money you had planned on using to buy your *biglietto d'autobus* (bus ticket) to Pompeii.

La morale of the story? Don't sit down to eat if you don't plan on eating. Even if it will empty your pockets, pick up the tab yourself. You'll make a lot of friends quickly and you'll leave Italy having made una *bella figura* (a good impression).

EAT LIKE AN ITALIAN
MANGIARE COME UN ITALIANO

Even if you consider yourself a veteran eater of *la cucina italiana* (Italian cuisine), there are a few things you might want to keep in mind the next time you dine in Italy. Try to stay open-minded.

Don't ask for a doggy bag.

Don't be surprised if your date is mortified when you ask for a doggie bag. Italians never take doggie bags from a *ristorante* unless they actually have one of the four-legged guys back home; it's considered very gauche.

Don't snack.

Italians don't snack much, saving their *appetito* for the main meals. Otherwise, they would be the fattest people on Earth.

Lunch.

Italians used to sit down and have a meal that *mamma* or *nonna* had been cooking all day. Things have changed. Most working Italians grab a bite at the local bar, which is more like a café than a pub. What makes their bars different is the fact that they actually drink and eat, and there's more than some germ-ridden popcorn offered.

Wait!

Aspetta! When it comes to le feste like *Natale* and *Pasqua* (Easter), the old standards still apply. Try not to engulf everything you see, because more will be coming shortly. And more, and more, and more.

Get your own pizza!

In Italy, everyone orders their own pizza, which is the size of a plate and usually has only one or two toppings like *funghi* (mushrooms) or *pomodori* (tomatoes). You know those Round Table personal pizzas they sell at sports events? Think of those, but not made out of crap. P.S. Italians do not ask for extra cheese for their pizza and I won't even comment on the ranch dressing.

Cheese, please.

Many innocent Americans have had their minds blown upon discovering that Italians don't use gobs of melted *formaggio* (cheese) on every pasta dish served. This may also explain why Italians are in general lighter and brighter.

Espresso.

If you're drinking espresso in Italy, all you have to ask for is *un caffé*. Italians drink *cappuccino* for breakfast and sometimes as a pick-me-up in the afternoon, but never after a meal. (Only *turisti* do that.) Also, don't expect a little slice of lemon rind on the edge of your *demitasse* like you might have seen in a scene out of *The Sopranos*.

Picking up the tab.

If you're going out for *caffé* with friends, it's typical that one person picks up the tab this time. The other gets it next time. You'll look like un *tirchio*—a real cheap turd—if you start pulling out coins from the pockets of your sand-blasted jeans.

Sambuca.

Most Italians by habit do not order Sambuca after every meal, nor do they necessarily throw coffee beans in the drink like is typically done in just about every Italian-American *eatery* with a checkered tablecloth. But do indulge in a *digestivo* (digestif).

Bread.

There are as many different kinds of *pane* (bread) as there are dialects. *Il burro* (butter) is never served with bread. And don't expect to find a little dish of *olio d'oliva* for dipping either. *Il pane* is included with the cover charge.

I stuffed myself like a pig.
Mi sono abbuffato come un maiale.

I'm full.
Sono pieno/a.

·····Excuse me!
Mi scusi!

Snapping your fingers and yelling is far less effective than
a respectable *Mi scusi* when trying to get the attention of
your *cameriere* (waiter). And when the time comes to settle
up, remember that most Italian establishments don't bring
il conto (the bill) until you ask for it, and even then they'll
take their time.

Excuse me.
Mi scusi.

Can I have…?
Posso avere…?

> **the menu**
> *la lista*
>
> **a fork**
> *una forchetta*
>
> **a knife**
> *un coltello*
>
> **a spoon**
> *un cucchiaio*

What are we eating?
Cosa mangiamo?

I could eat you for dinner.
*Potrei mangiarti per la **cena**.*

We'd like to order, thanks.
*Vorremo **ordinare**, grazie.*

We're in a rush.
Abbiamo fretta.

What are you doing later on?
Che cosa fai più tardi?
If your waiter or waitress is cute, why not give it a shot?

What do you recommend?
*Che cosa **raccomanda**?*

What's in this dish?
*Di che cosa consiste questo **piatto**?*

Can you bring the check, please.
*Ci porti il **conto**, per favore.*

Did you leave a tip?
*Hai lasciato una **mancia**?*
Leaving *una mancia* is optional, since you're paying *il coperto* (a cover charge) for both the service and the *pane*, but it's cool to leave a little extra something.

·····How gross!
Che schifo!

Uttered by millions every day, *Che schifo!* literally translates to "How gross!" The noun *uno schifo* refers to "a gross thing" and can be easily changed to the adjective *schifoso* (gross, or disgusting). The verbiage *fare schifo* is used to indicate something or someone of inferior quality, as in "it sucks."

That was awful!
*Era **pessimo**!*

That meal was crap.
*Quel pasto era di **merda**.*

That restaurant has *the worst service*.
*Quel ristorante ha **un servizio proprio sgarbato**.*

That restaurant sucked.
Il ristorante era uno schifo.

The idea of eating horsemeat turns my stomach.
*L'idea di mangiare la carne di cavallo **mi dà allo stomaco**.*

A dog wouldn't eat this.
Non lo mangerebbe neanche un cane.

I found a hair in my pasta.
Ho trovato un capello nella pasta.

This is so bland.
Questo non ha né amore né sapore.
Literally, "This has neither love nor taste." Notice the rhyme.

This has a nasty taste.
*Questo ha un **sapore cattivo**.*

If you ask me, this is a plate of shit.
Secondo me, questo piatto è proprio di merda.

This'll make you vomit.
Questo è da vomitare.

Too many cooks spoil the broth.
*Troppi cuochi **guastano** la cucina.*

·····Pasta puttanesca?
Pasta puttanesca?

It's time to have a *spaghettata* with your friends. *Spaghettata* is a uniquely Italian slang word that describes a meal that is spontaneously thrown together for a group of friends. All you need is a *bottiglia di vino* (a bottle of wine) served alongside a steaming bowl of home-cooked pasta *puttanesca*.

A little background about this *piatto* ("dish"), which originated in Napoli. Pasta *puttanesca* (literally, "whore pasta") got its name from the local prostitutes—the *puttane*— because it was fast, cheap, and spicy. Not to mention yummy. For those of you who are all thumbs in the kitchen, it's hard to mess this one up.

1 small onion, chopped
una cipolla, tritata

a little olive oil
un po' d'olio d'oliva

2 cloves of garlic
2 spicchi d'aglio

4 anchovies, chopped
4 acciughe, tritate

2 chile peppers
2 peperoncini

a handful of capers
dei capperi

a handful of black olives
delle olive

a small can of tomato sauce
un piccolo contenitore di pomodori pelati

a pinch of salt
un pizzico di sale

a pinch of black pepper
un pizzico di pepe

Italian parsley, chopped
il prezzemolo, tritato

a box of spaghetti
una scatola di spaghetti

Cook the onion in the olive oil on medium-high heat until it begins to caramelize. Add the garlic and anchovies and cook for a minute. Add the remaining ingredients except the spaghetti and the parsley and bring to a boil. Reduce the heat and simmer uncovered for 10 minutes, stirring occasionally.

While the sauce is simmering, cook the pasta. Make sure you don't overcook it; Italians eat their pasta *al dente* (literally, "to the tooth"), chewy like steak. Drain the cooked pasta. Gently stir the pasta and sauce together and sprinkle with chopped parsley.

As a variation, you can add a can of tuna fish to the sauce at the end, warming it—but not cooking (or it will taste fishy)—with the other *ingredienti* (ingredients).

·····Carnival of delights
Il carnevale dei delitti

Not inclined to waste, Italians will eat just about anything. You name it, and there's a dish for it. Treats include *trippa* (tripe), *puzzone* (stinky cheese), and *schienale* (spinal cord), to name just a few. The play on words in many of these delectables shouldn't be overlooked. Watch for these *specialità* the next time you're reading a menu.

STARTERS , SIDES, AND SOUPS
Gli antipasti e i contorni

Funghi porcini (pig mushrooms)
Plump and meaty mushrooms that look like little pigs.

Puzzone (big stink)
A particularly fragrant cheese.

Sopa caôda
A Venetian soup consisting of pigeon and cabbage.

Zuppa di piscialetto (piss-in-the-bed soup)
Italians don't mince words; made from dandelions, this soup is known for its diuretic effect.

FIRST COURSES
I primi & i sughi

Frittata (fried)
An omelette. When you say *Che frittata!* it means a real mess.

Pasta alla diavola (devil style)
Pasta with a spicy tomato sauce.

Sigaretti (cigarettes)
A cigarette-shaped pasta.

Ricci di donna (ladies' curls)
A very curly type of pasta.

Strozzapreti/strangolapreti (strangle-the-priest pasta)
A hand-rolled noodle that resembles the rope once used to hang criminals and other deviants.

MAIN COURSES
I secondi

Culatello (big ass)
Cured pork rump.

Gallinaccio (ugly rooster)
Turkey cock. Yup.

Le virtù (the virtues)
A dish involving seven ingredients representing seven virgins. In myth it was claimed to be a powerful aphrodisiac.

Monacone (fat monk)
With its layers of eggplant, veal, prosciutto, tomato, and fontina cheese, this dish has enough calories to last a winter, hence the name.

Pastissada di cavallo (horse slop)
A stew made from horsemeat served with polenta.

Pollo alla diavola (devil's chicken)
Chicken that is heavily seasoned, usually with chile peppers or black pepper.

Quinto quarto (fifth quarter)
This refers to the organs, brains, hooves, and testicles of a butchered animal.

Rana pescatrice (frog fish)
Monkfish; this guy is one ugly friggin' fish.

Stighiole
Grilled lamb guts, a popular Sicilian street food.

Saltimbocca (jump in the mouth)
A Roman specialty consisting of veal, prosciutto, and sage, sautéed in butter; it takes about the same time to prepare as a hamburger but provides infinitely greater satisfaction.

Trippa (tripe)
Eating tripe is sort of like eating rubber bands drenched in tomato sauce.

Vastedda
Stewed spleen sandwich, a Sicilian treat.

SWEETS
I dolci

Addormenta suocere (sleeping mothers-in-law)
Candied nuts that supposedly send mothers-in-law off into a deep sleep.

Fave dei morti (dead men's beans)
Fava bean–shaped cookies eaten on All Soul's Day, November 2.

Lingue di gatto (cat tongues)
Thin butter cookies.

Minne di Sant'Agata (St. Agatha's nipples)
Breast-shaped cookies honoring the martyr St. Agatha.

Ossi di morti (dead men's bones)
A cookie molded in the shape of a shank bone. The name is somewhat redundant, but you get the picture.

Panettone della passione (big bread of passion)
A cakelike bread from Florence that's supposed to ignite the flames of love.

Stinchetti di morto (dead man's shins)
Bone-shaped Umbrian cookies.

Tiramisù (pick-me-up)
Made from espresso, ladyfingers, and mascarpone, along with a dash of rum. You'll be flying in no time.

Tre mosche (three flies)
Refers to the coffee beans occasionally dropped into Sambuca that look like—you guessed it—flies.

Vin santo (holy wine)
A sweet wine, super high in alcohol, likely to bring anyone to a near ecstatic state; usually consumed during dessert.

·····Acknowledgments

The author gratefully acknowledges all the people at Ulysses Press, in particular Alice Riegert for her terrific editing of this book, Lindsay Mack for her illustrations, Lauren Harrison for copyediting, and Abigail Reser for production.

Special thanks to Laura Anson for her insights about "things Italian" and for her help with researching this book. I don't know what I would have done without readers like Cristina Melotti and Lorenza Cerbini. *Grazie* to Peter Mielnicki for waking up from the dead; to Frank Mongardi for his passion of words; and to my *studenti* at our weekly "salon," where we eat, drink *vino*, and conjugate verbs while discussing inflectives. Grazie to the gang at 1644, to Stacy and Alberto Guglielmi, GP Roseghini, *la famigila* Destilo, Kim Malcolm, *la famiglia* Salamone (especially Marc!), Frank and Gail Duncan, Nina Jecker-Burn, and to my brother, Robert, for giving me ample opportunities to practice using the material in this book.

And a gazillion *baci* to Sabine, for making me laugh every day.

·····About the author

Gabrielle Euvino is an instructor of Italian and has written numerous books about the Italian language, including *The Complete Idiot's Guide to Learning Italian* and *The Pocket Idiot's Guide to Italian* (Alpha Books). She has been interviewed on Sirius Radio and profiled in newspaper and magazine articles.